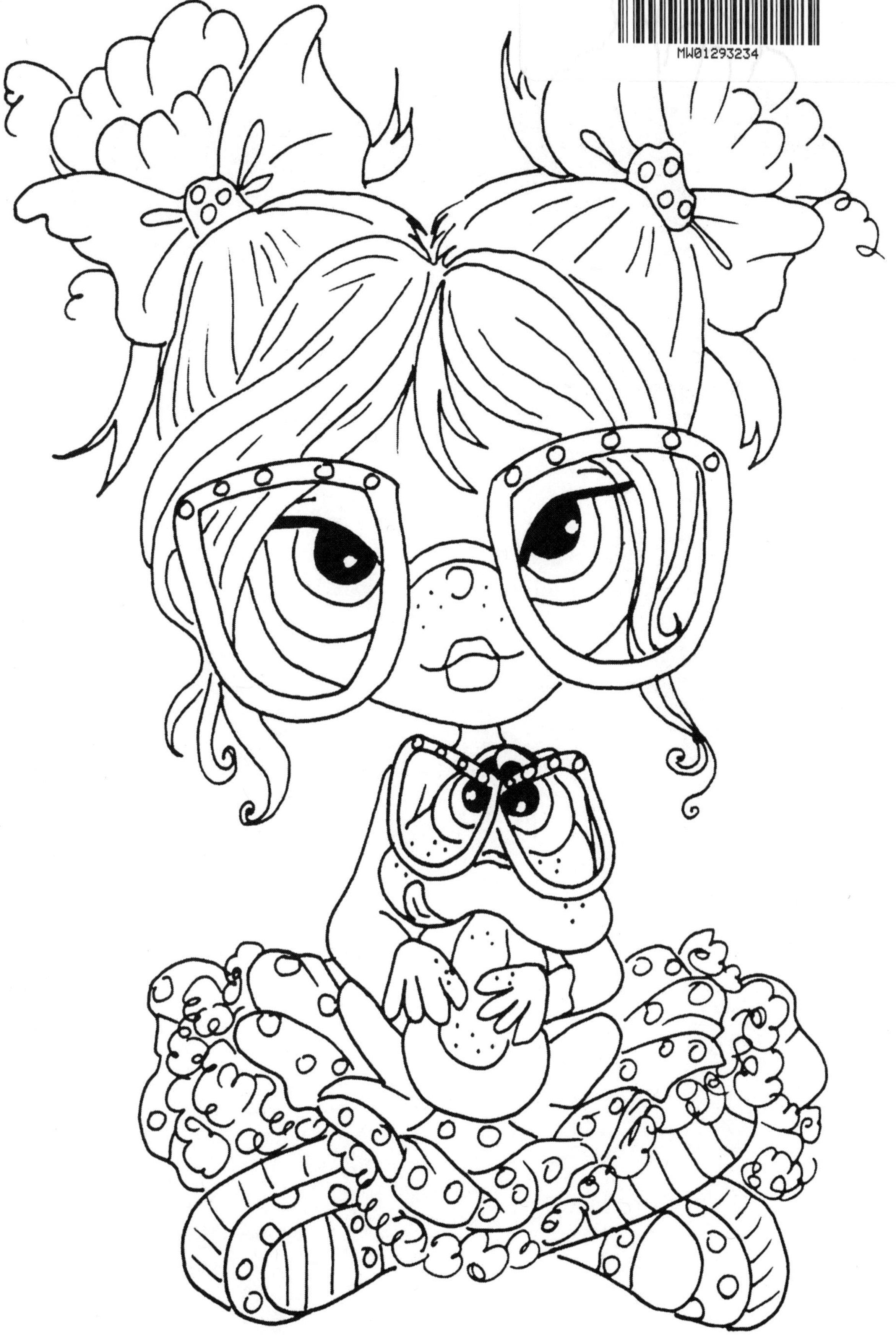

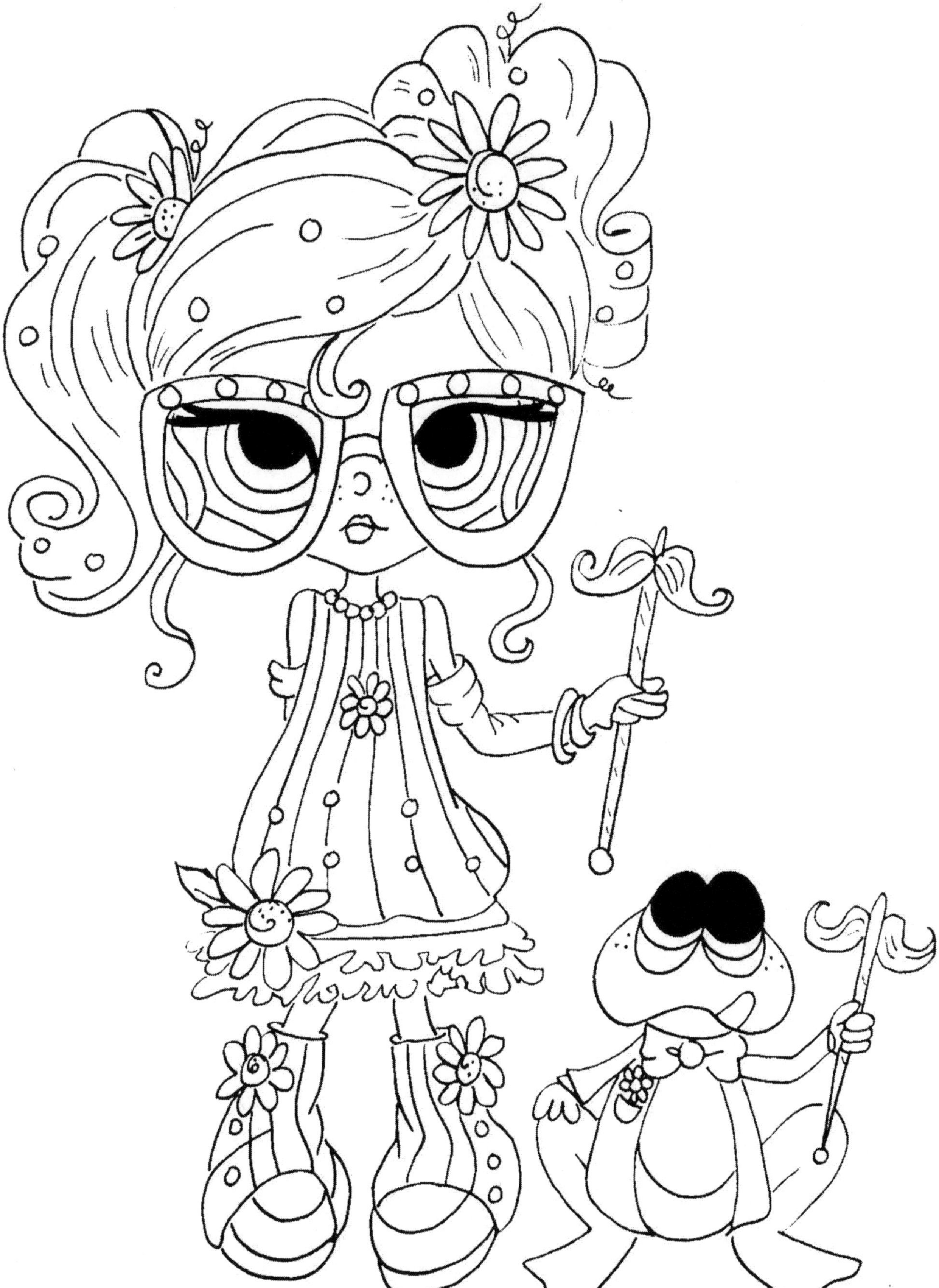

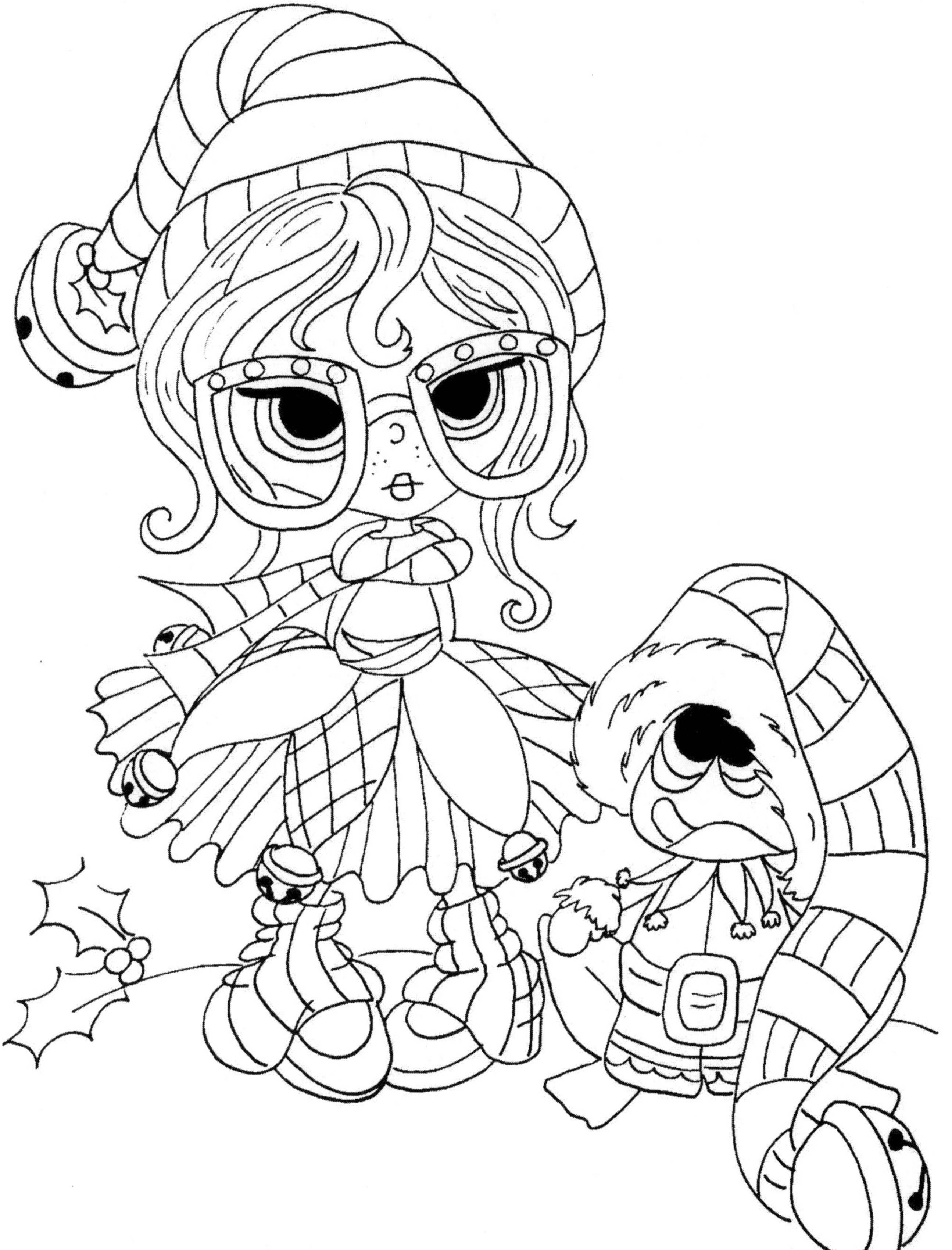

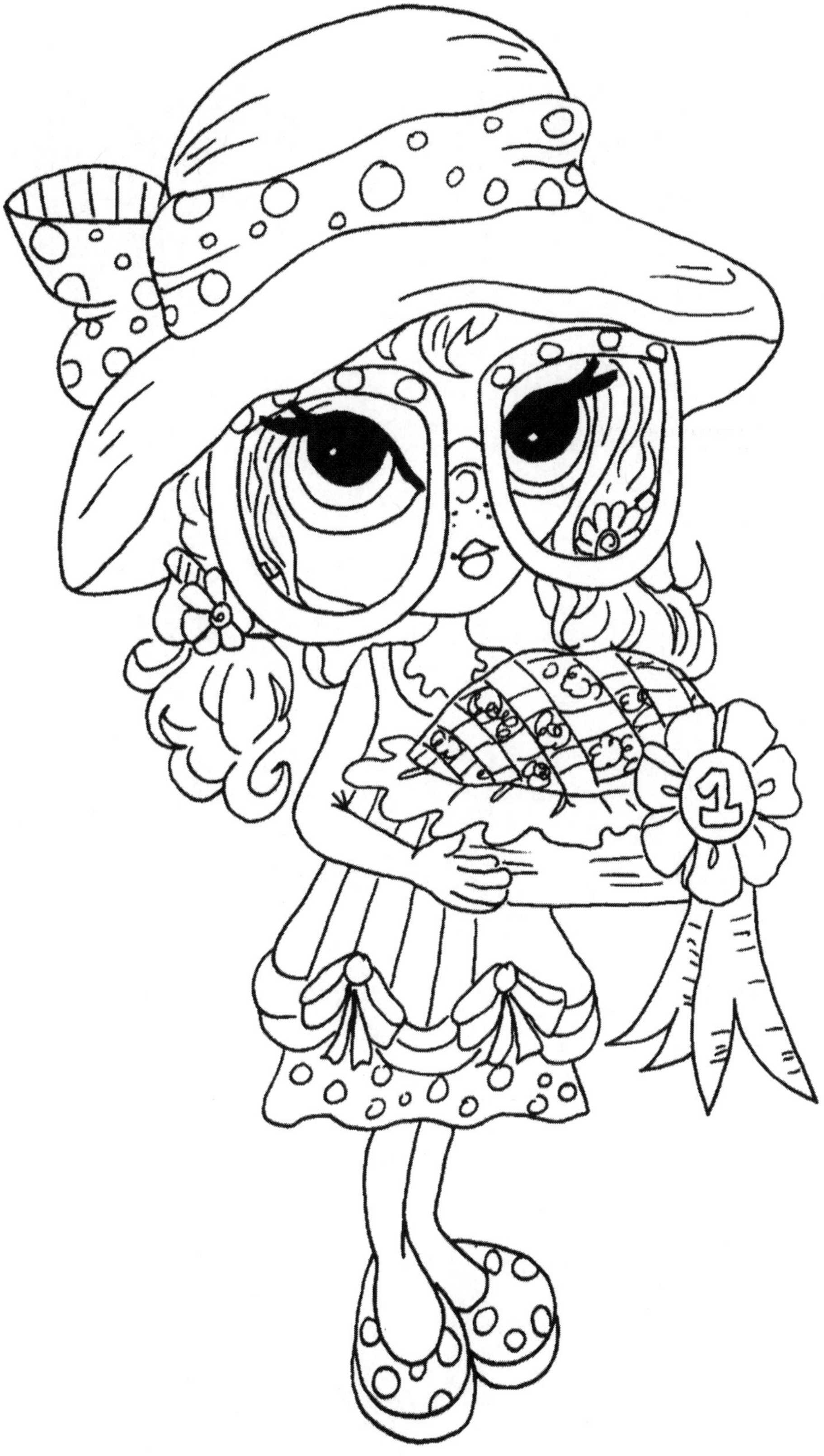
1

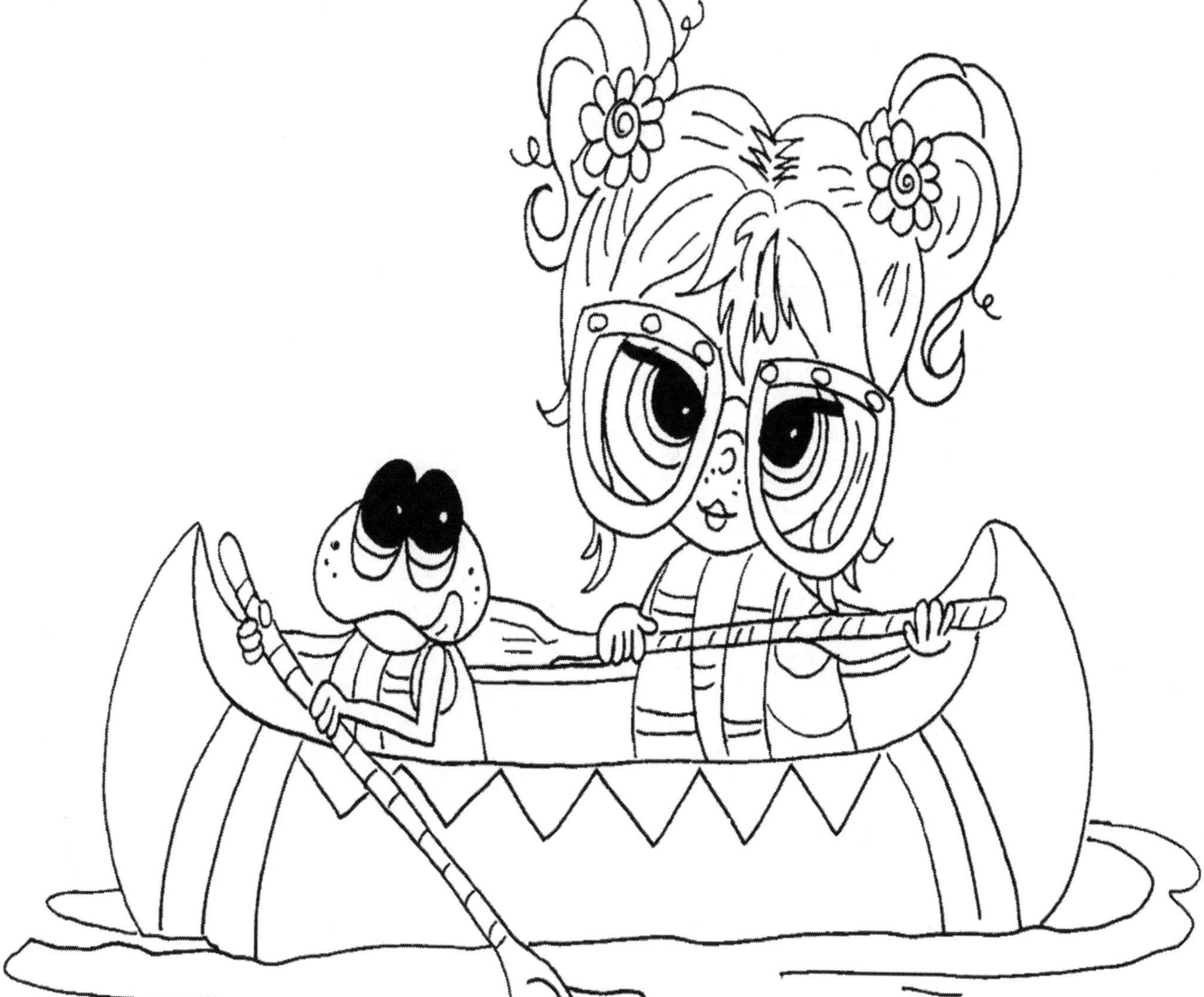

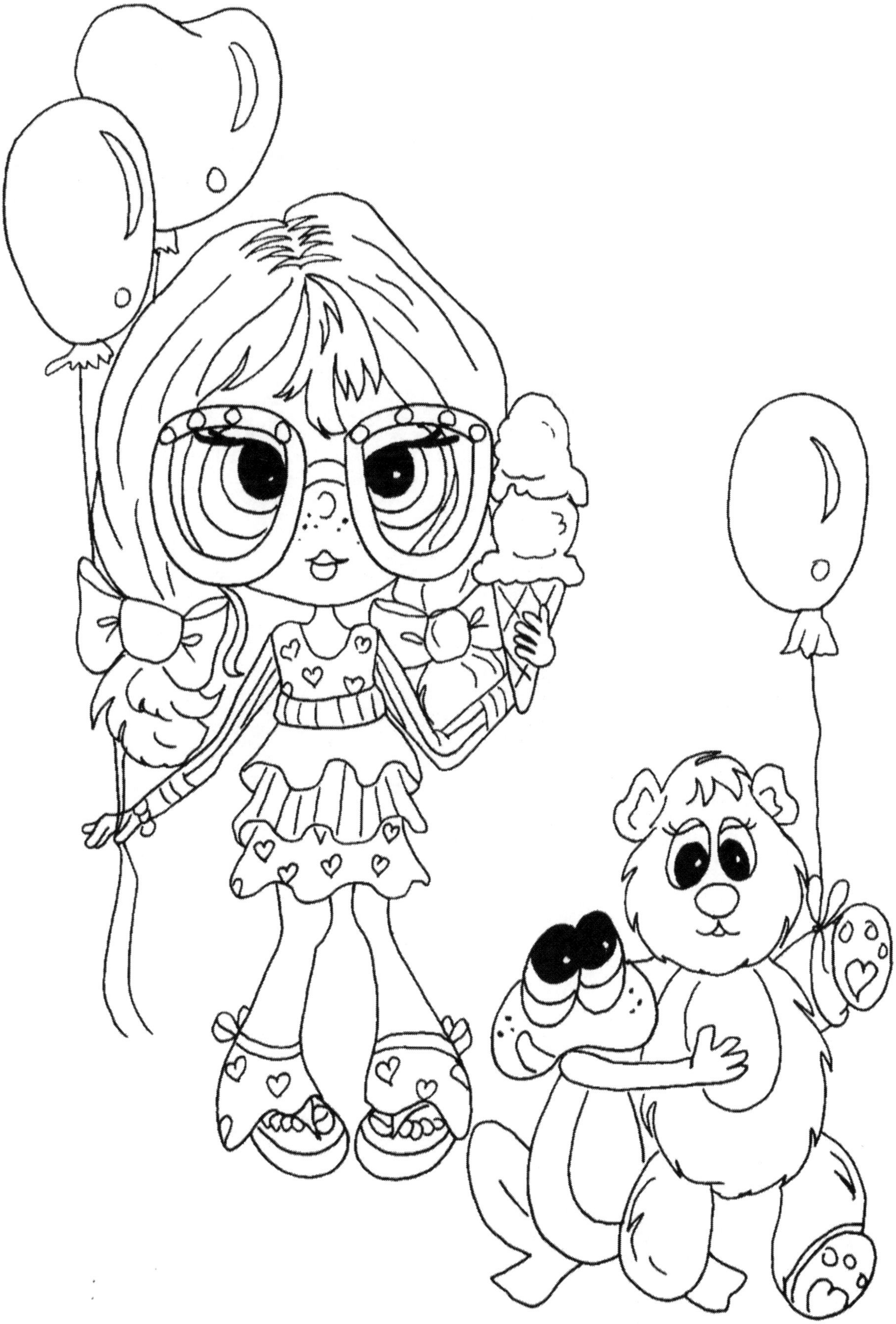

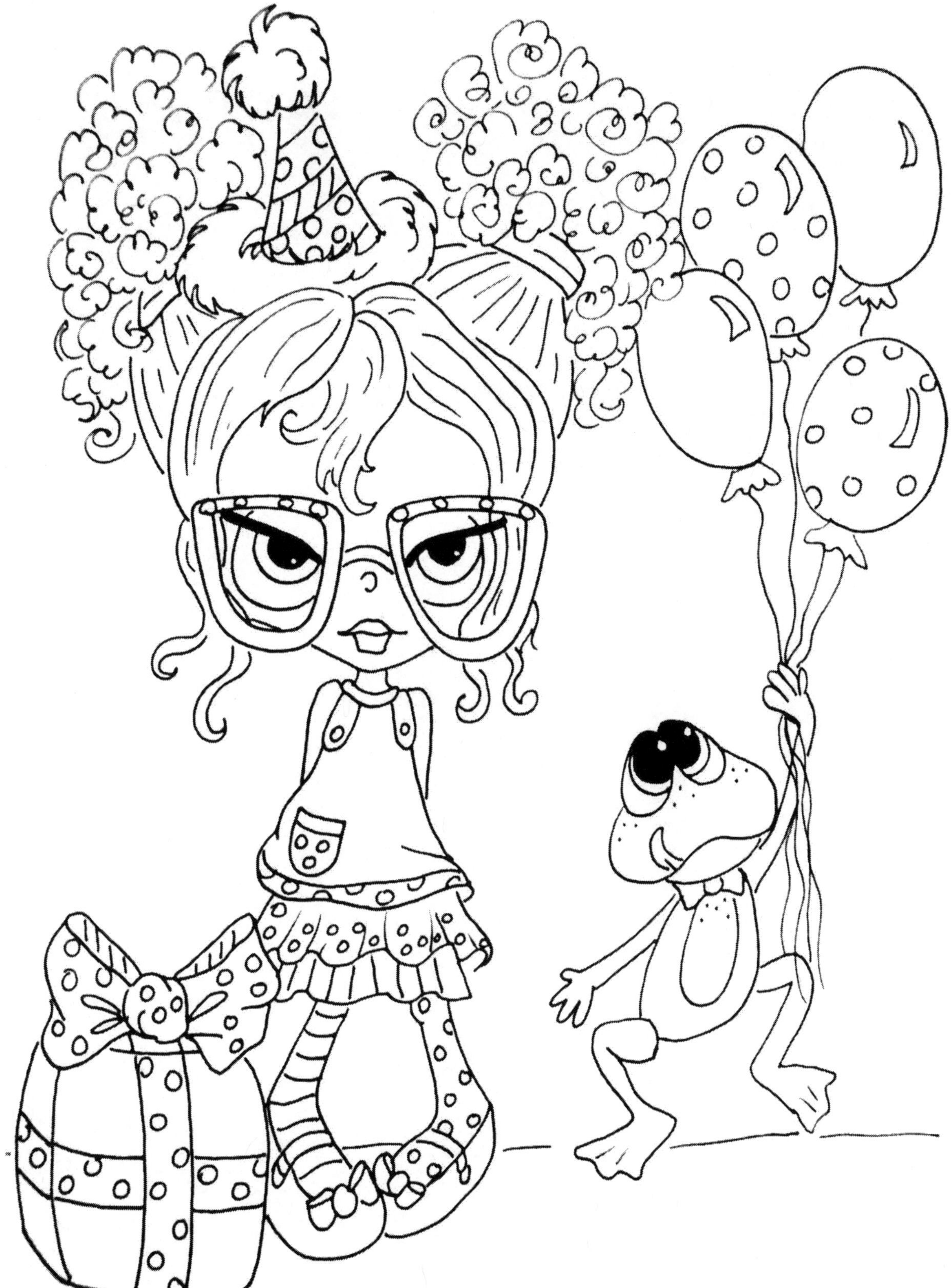

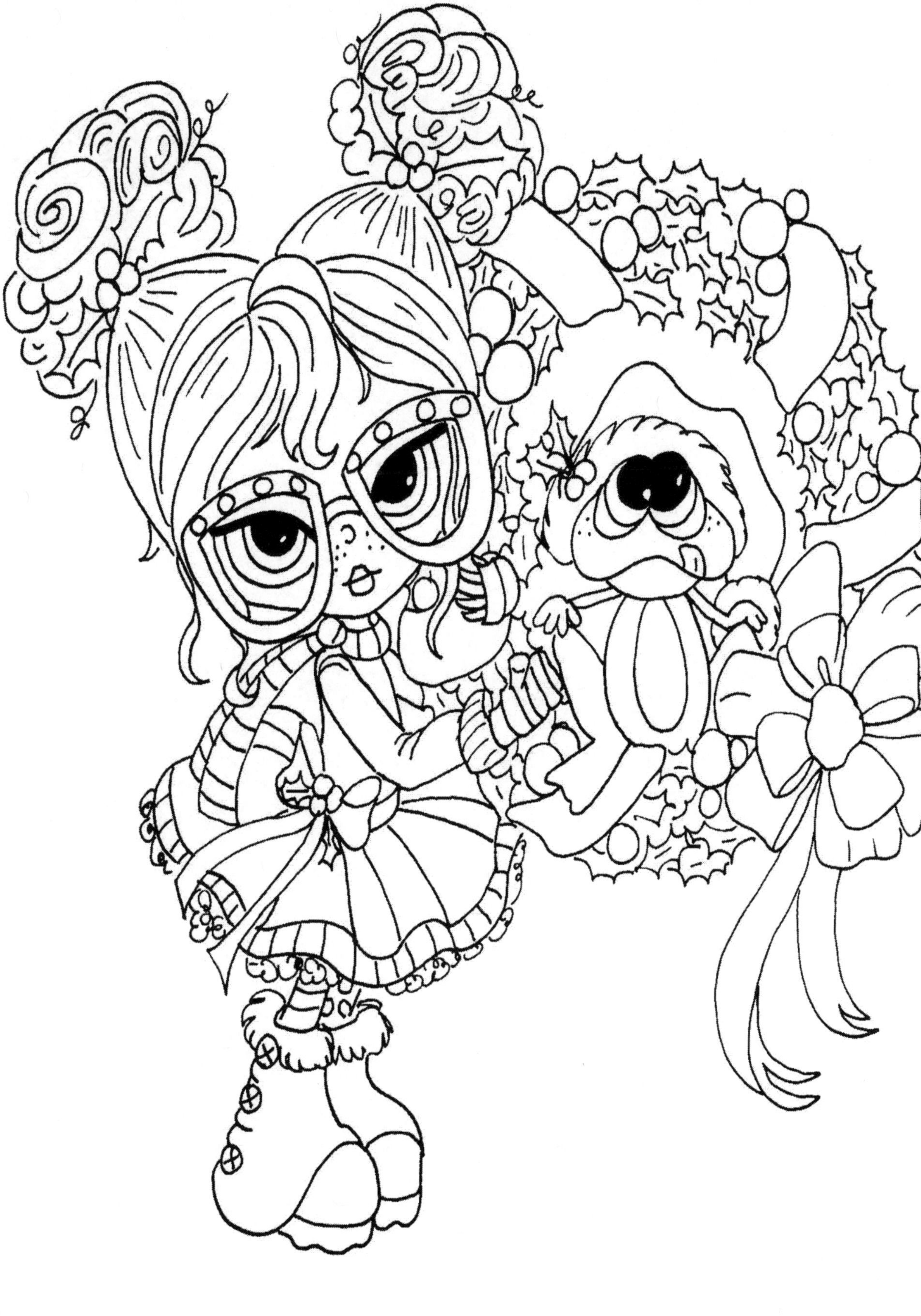

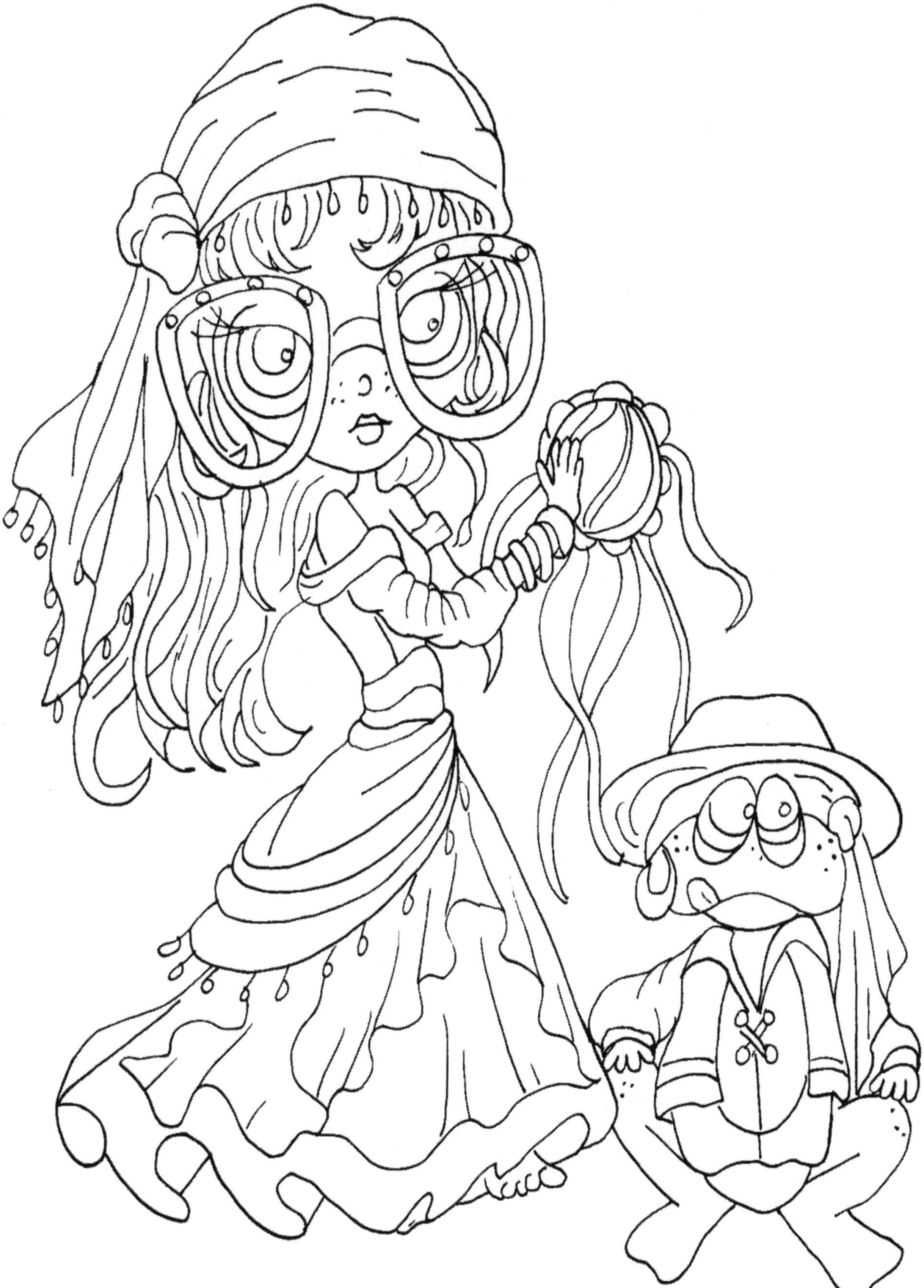

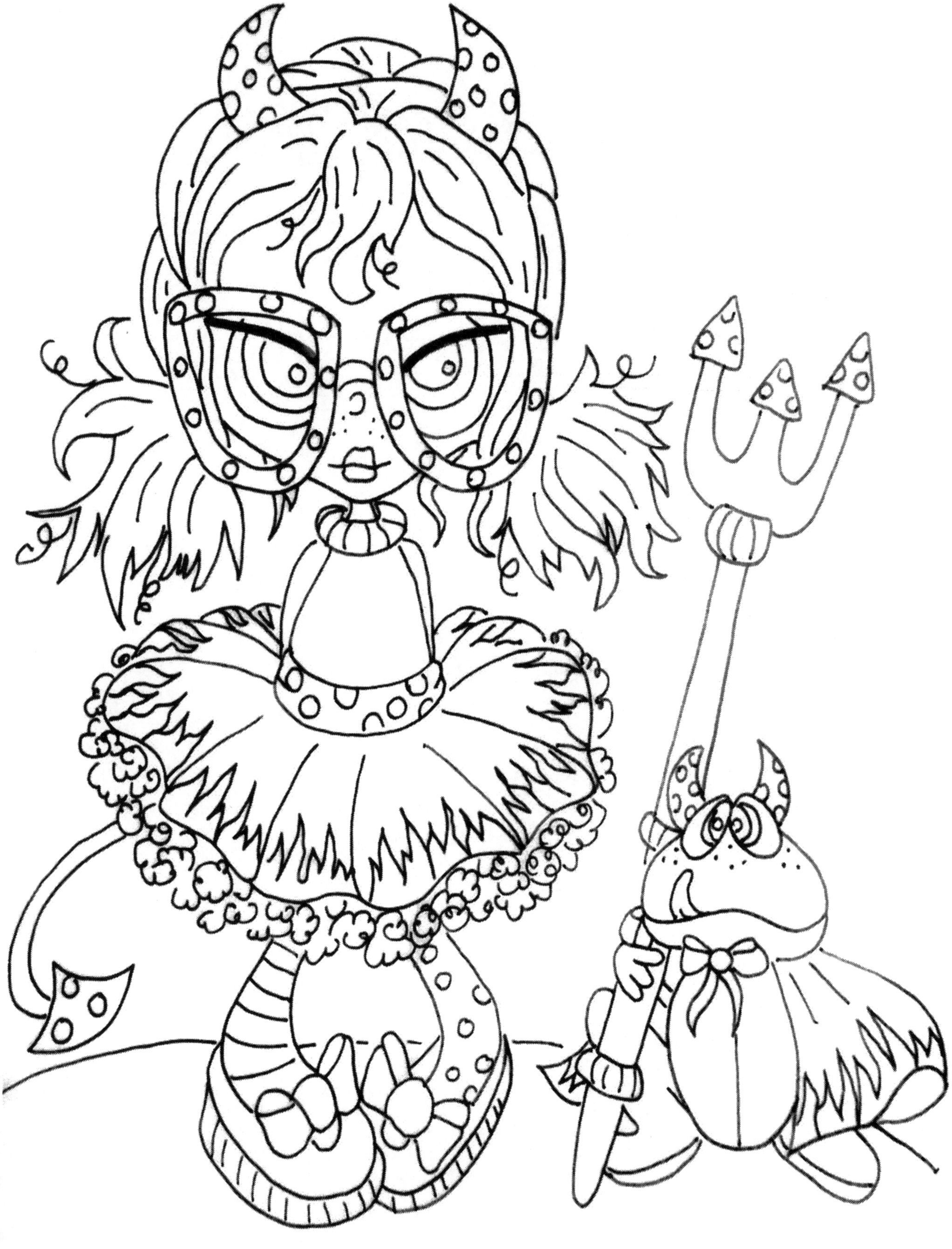

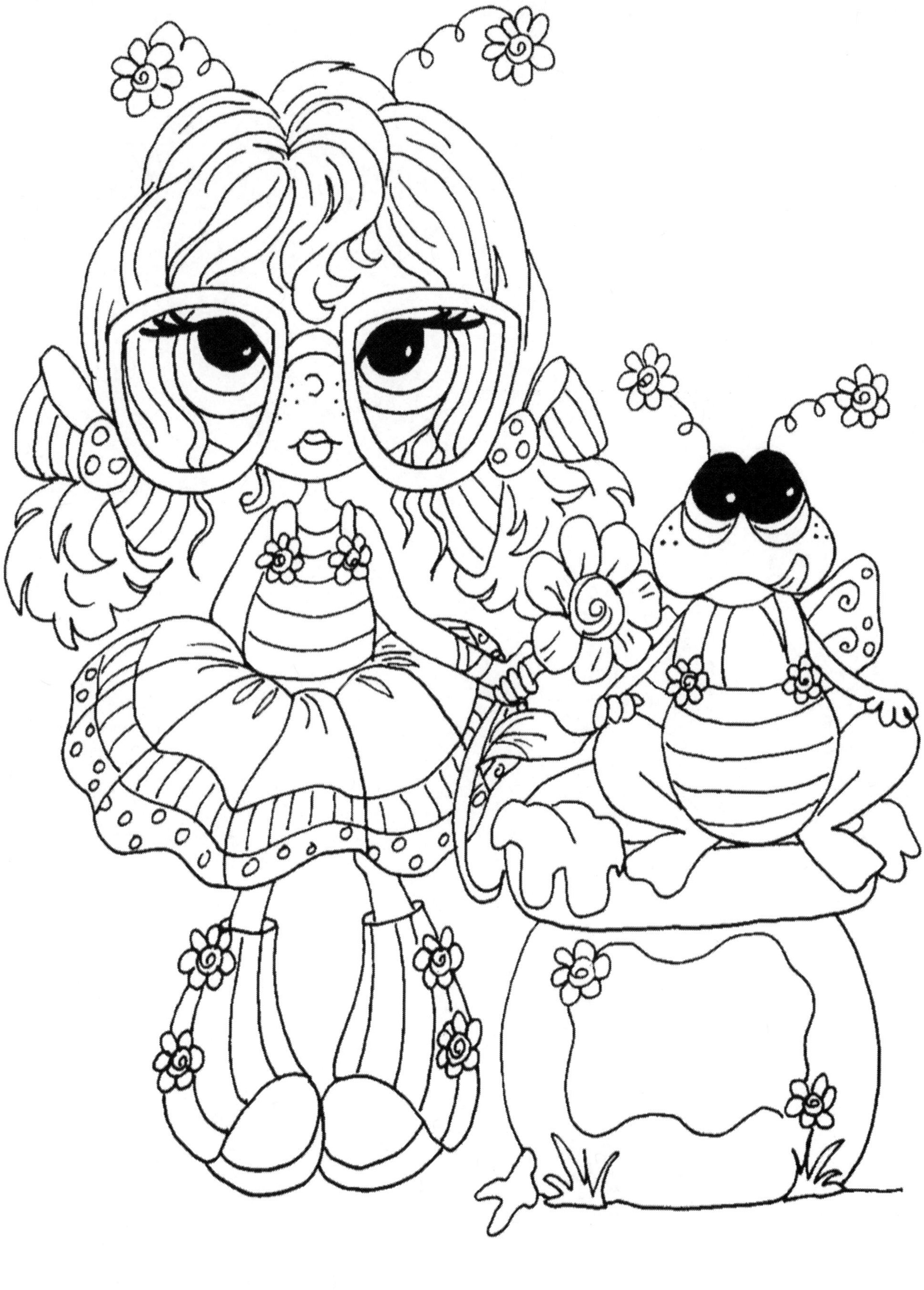

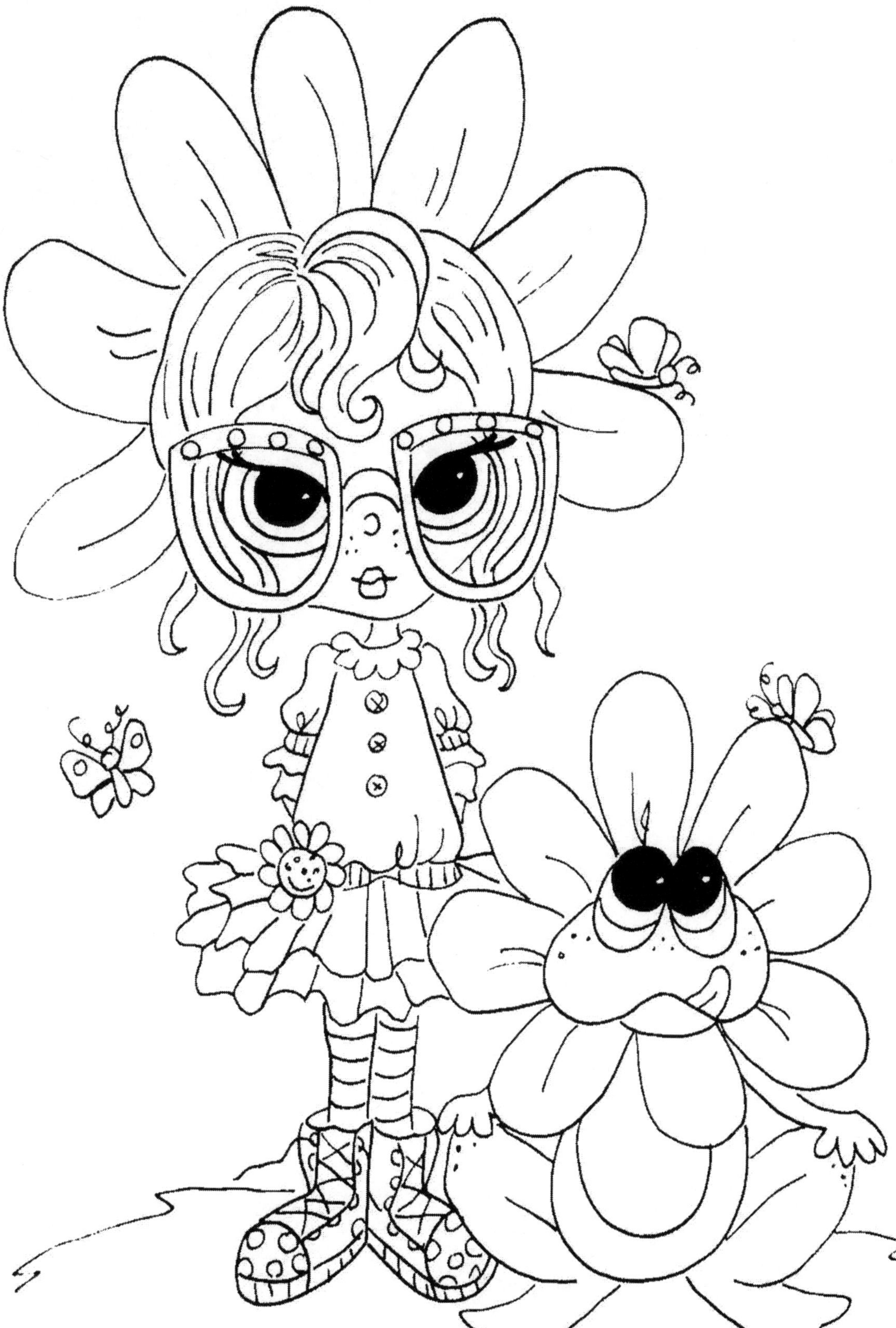

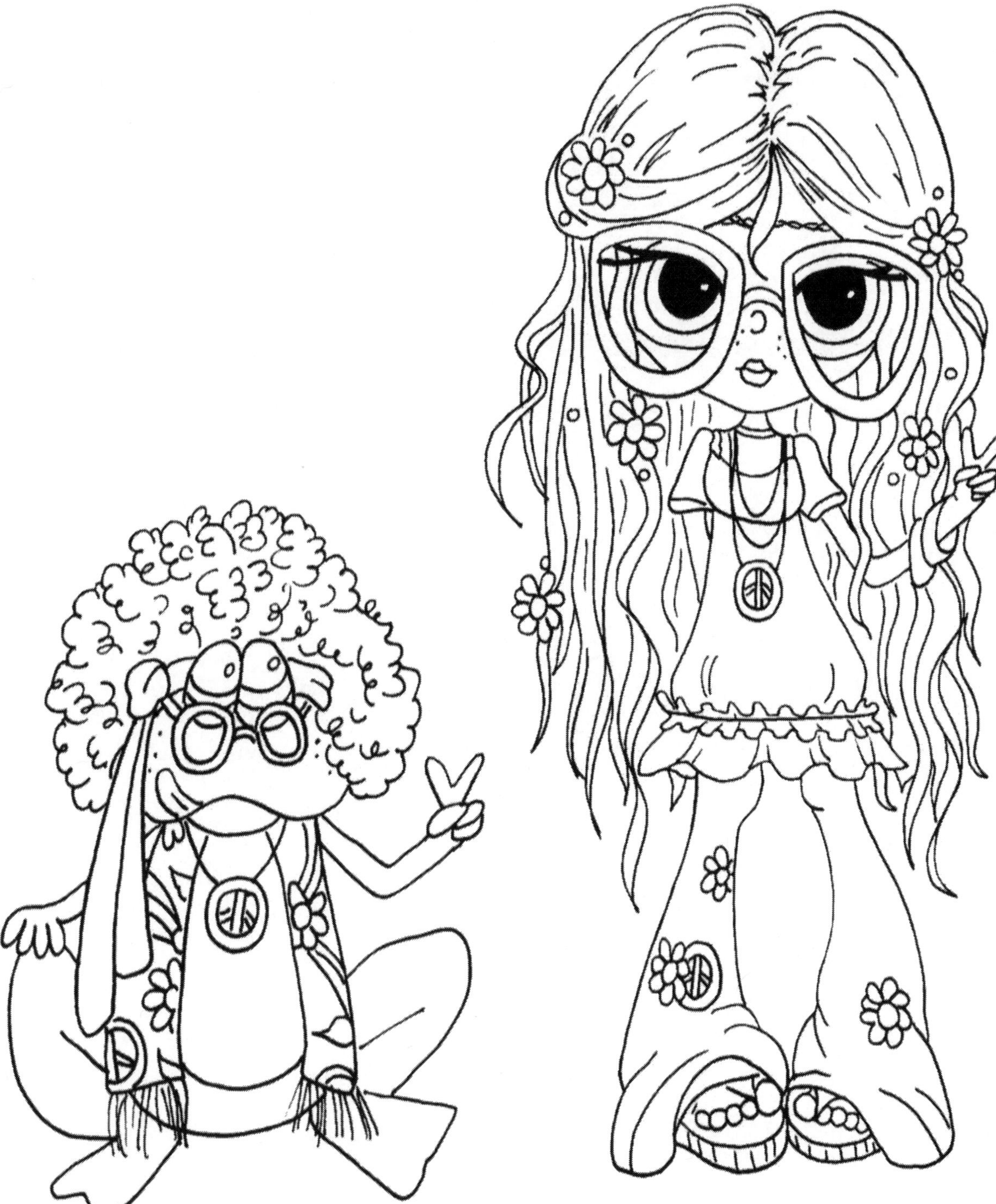

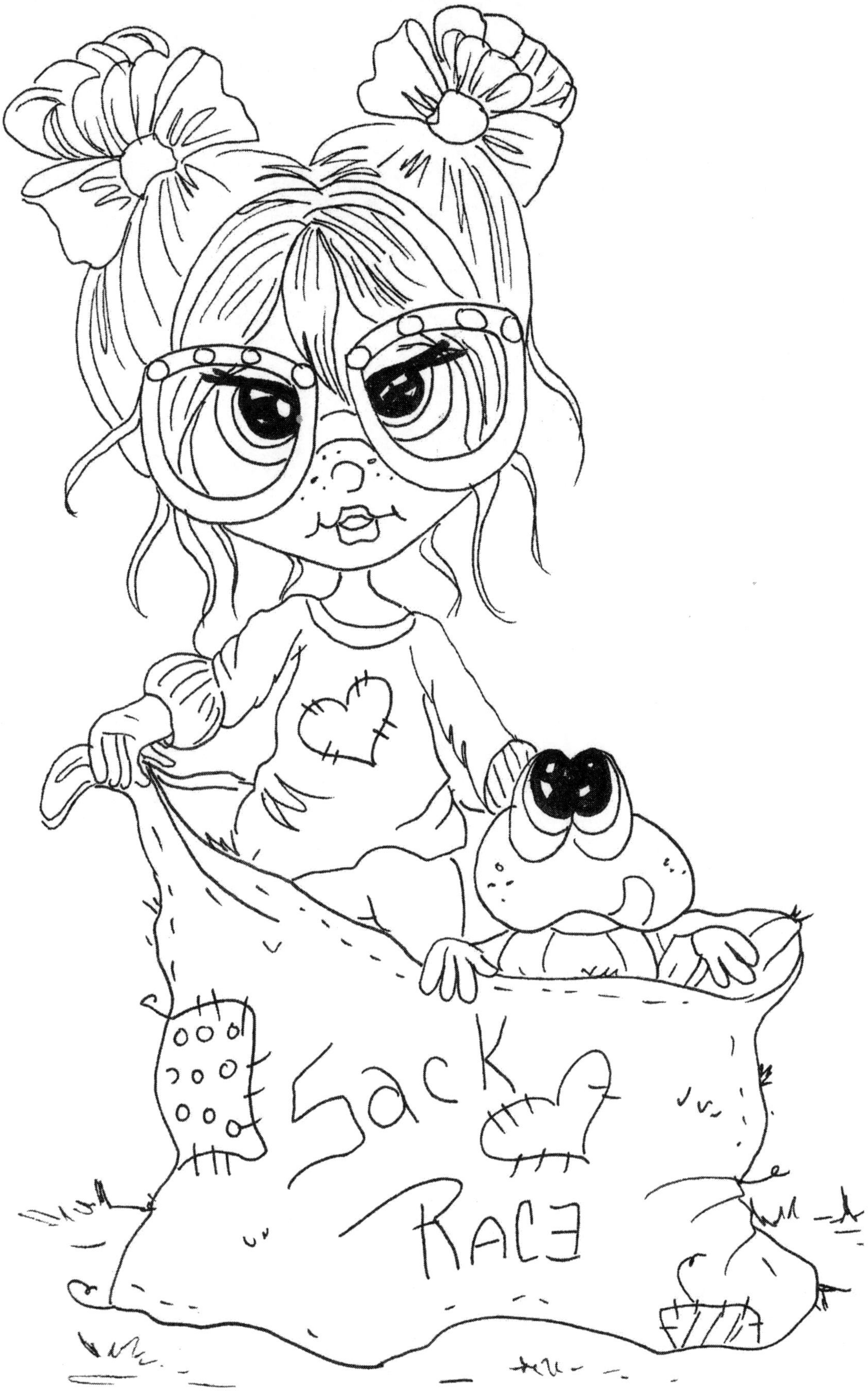
Sack
RACƎ

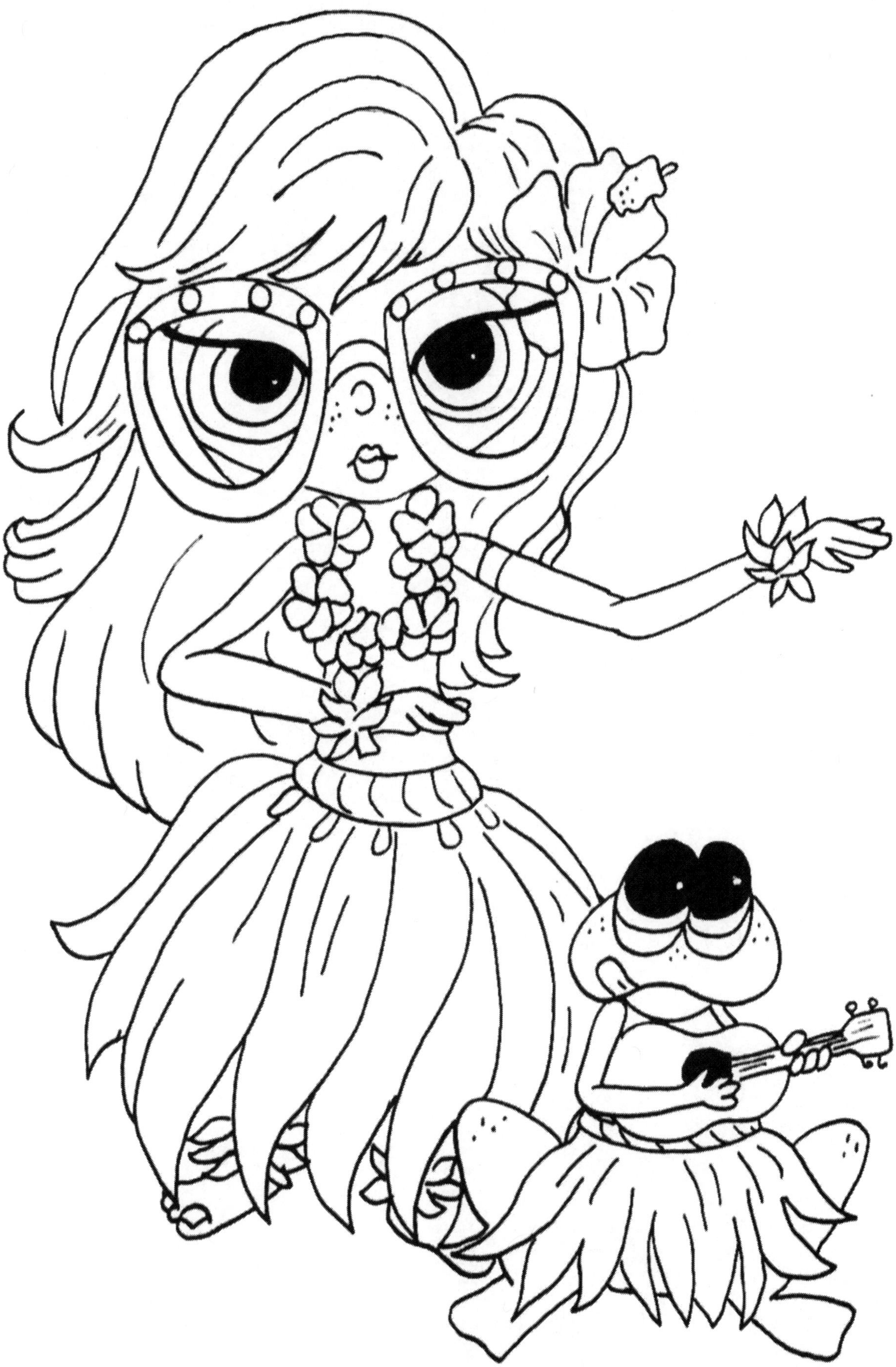

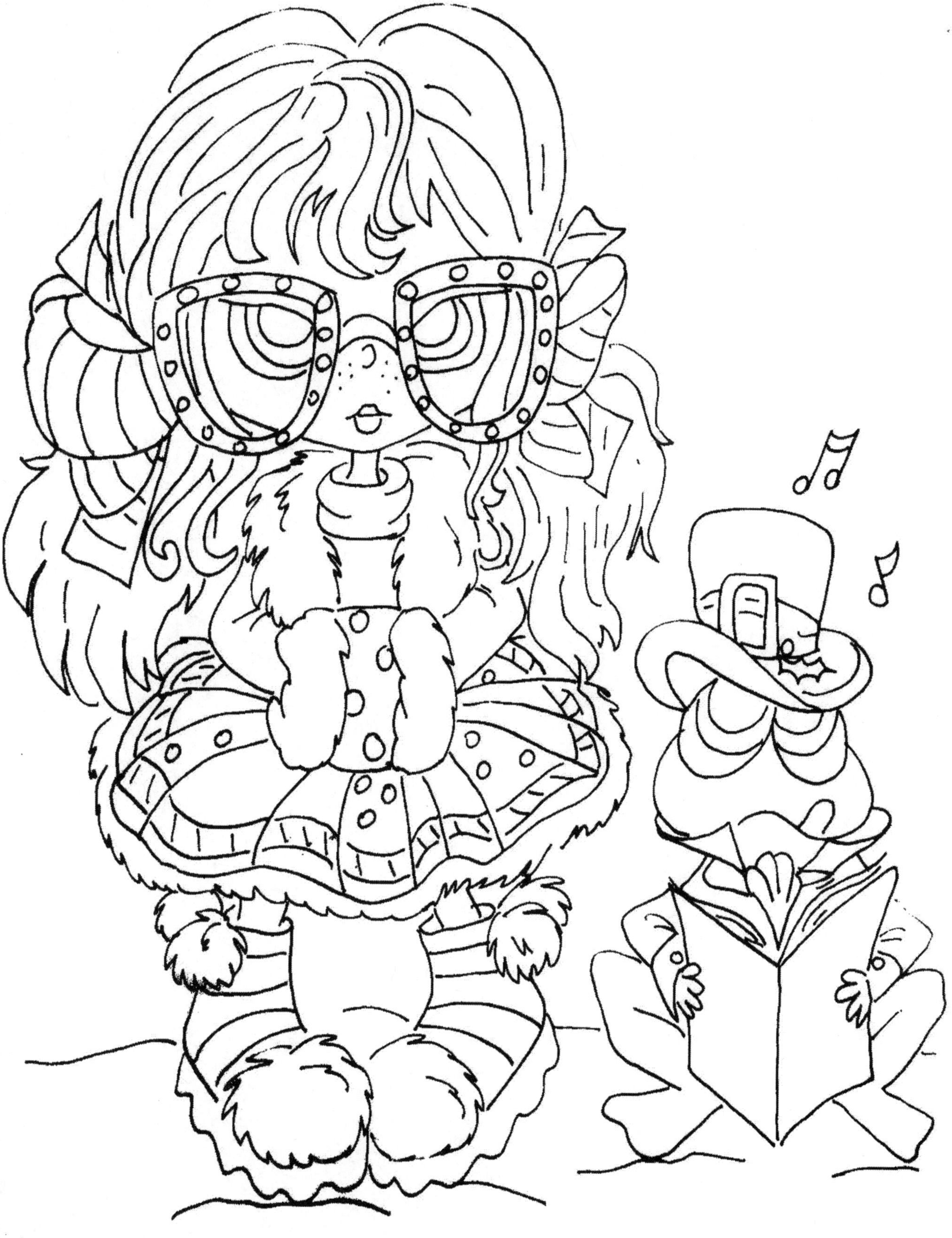

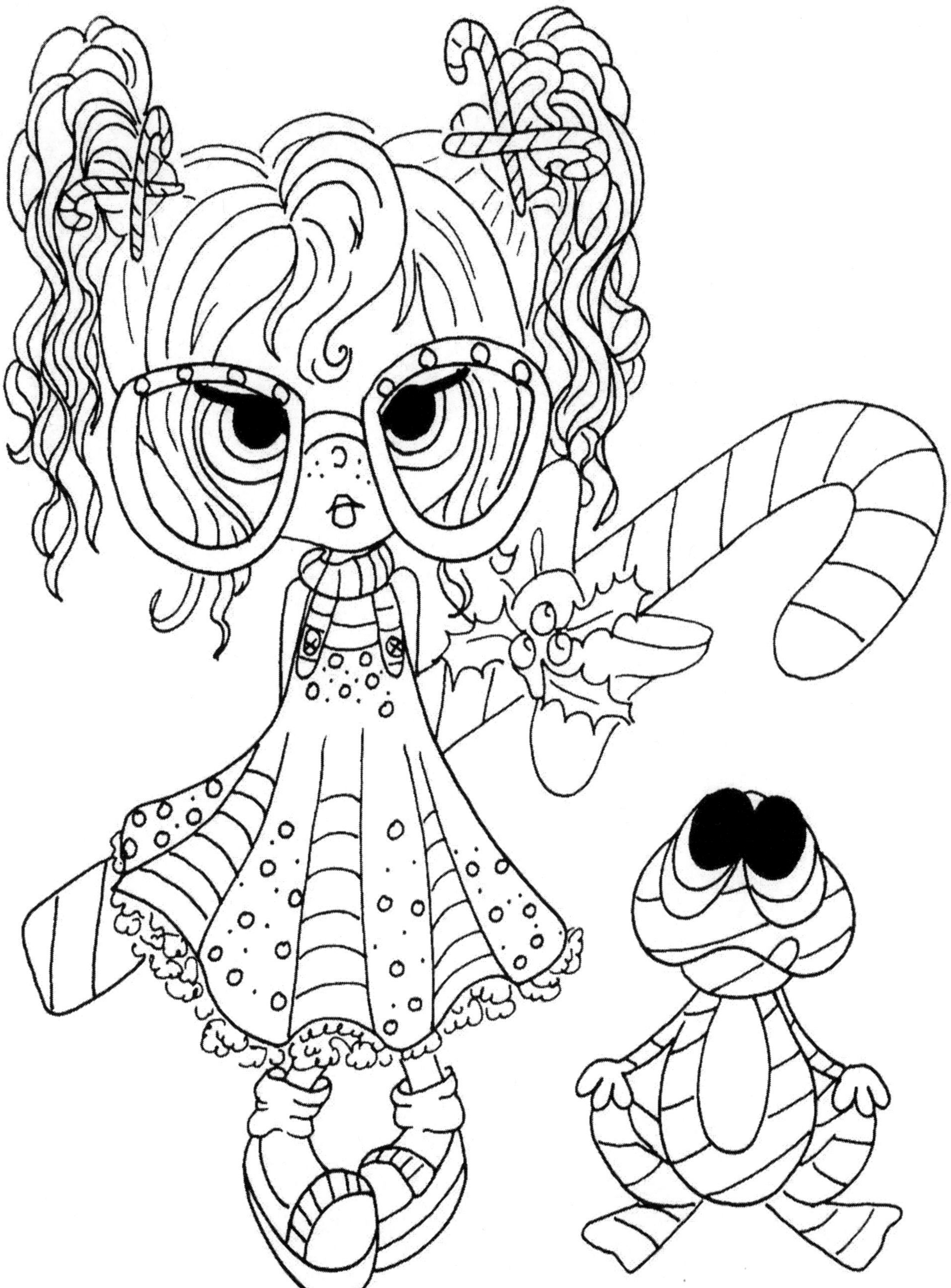

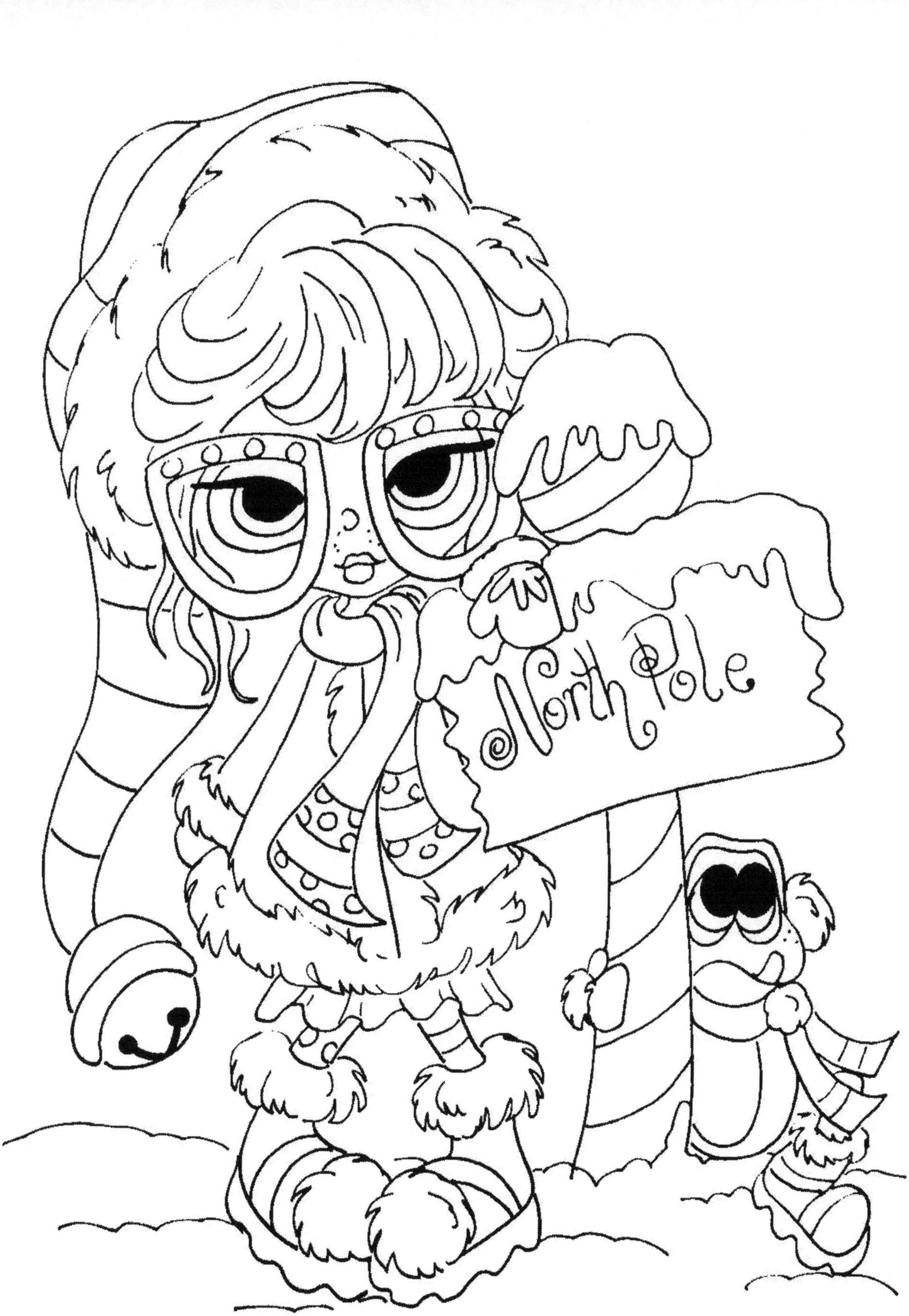
North Pole.

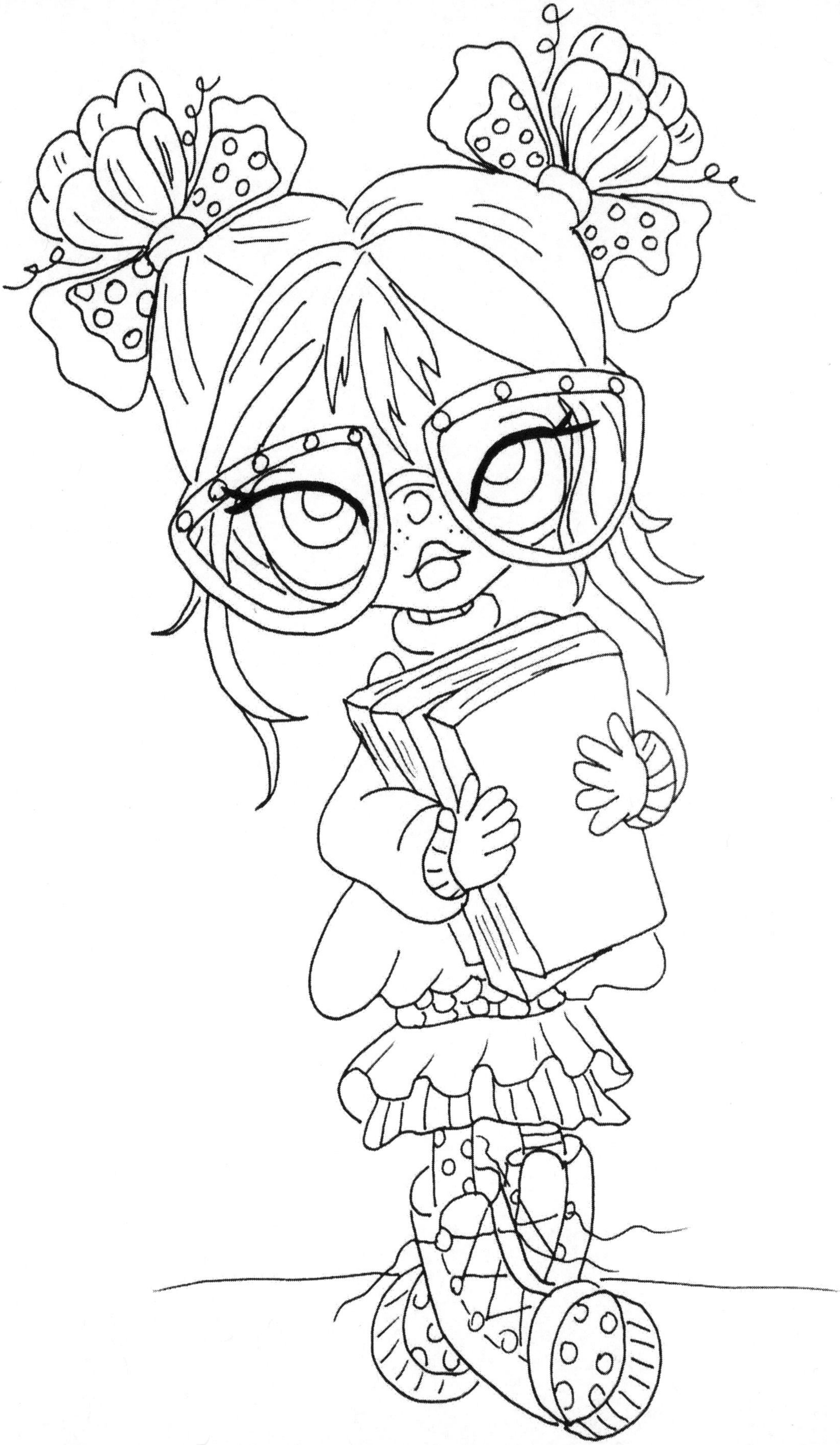

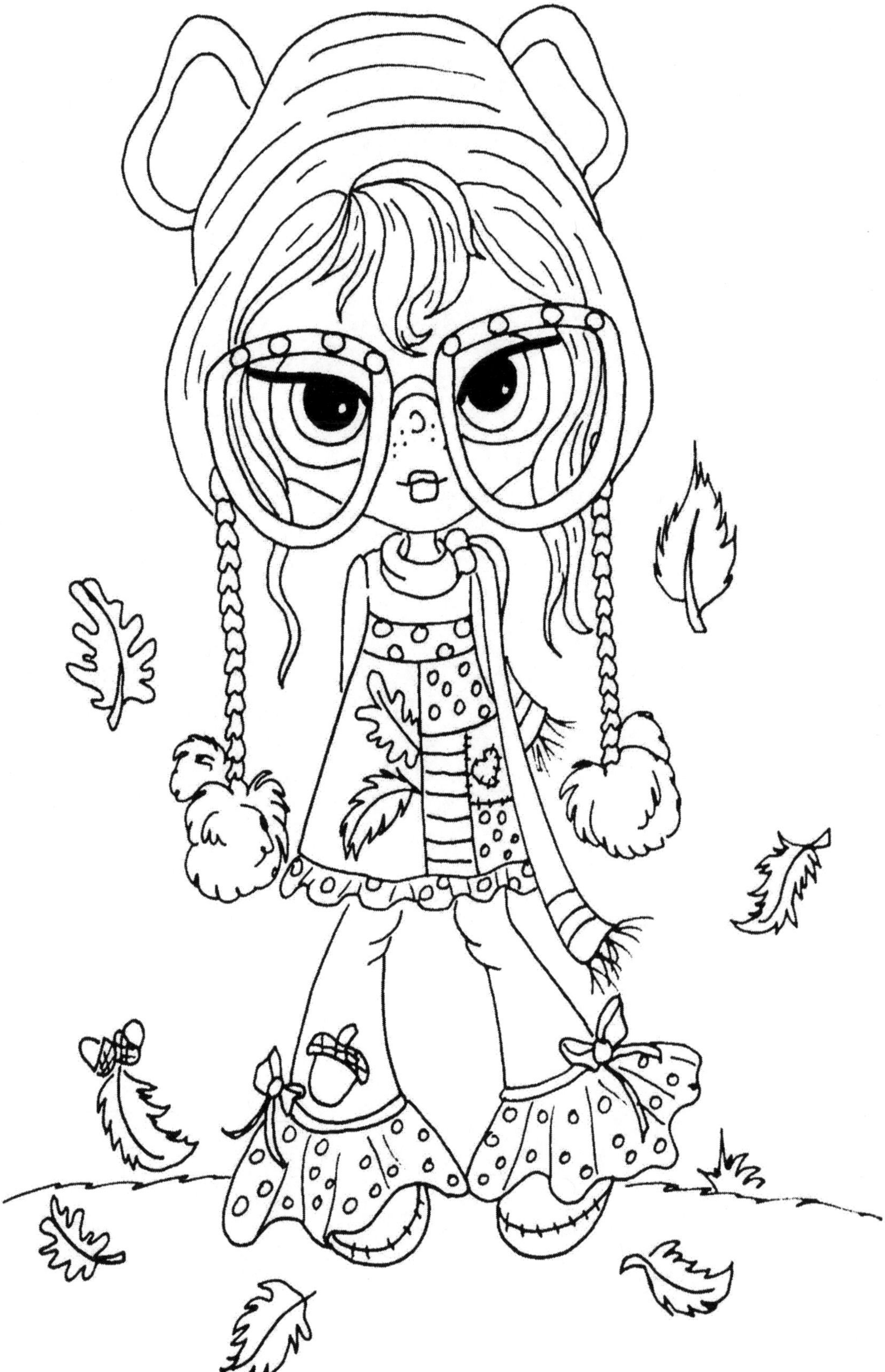

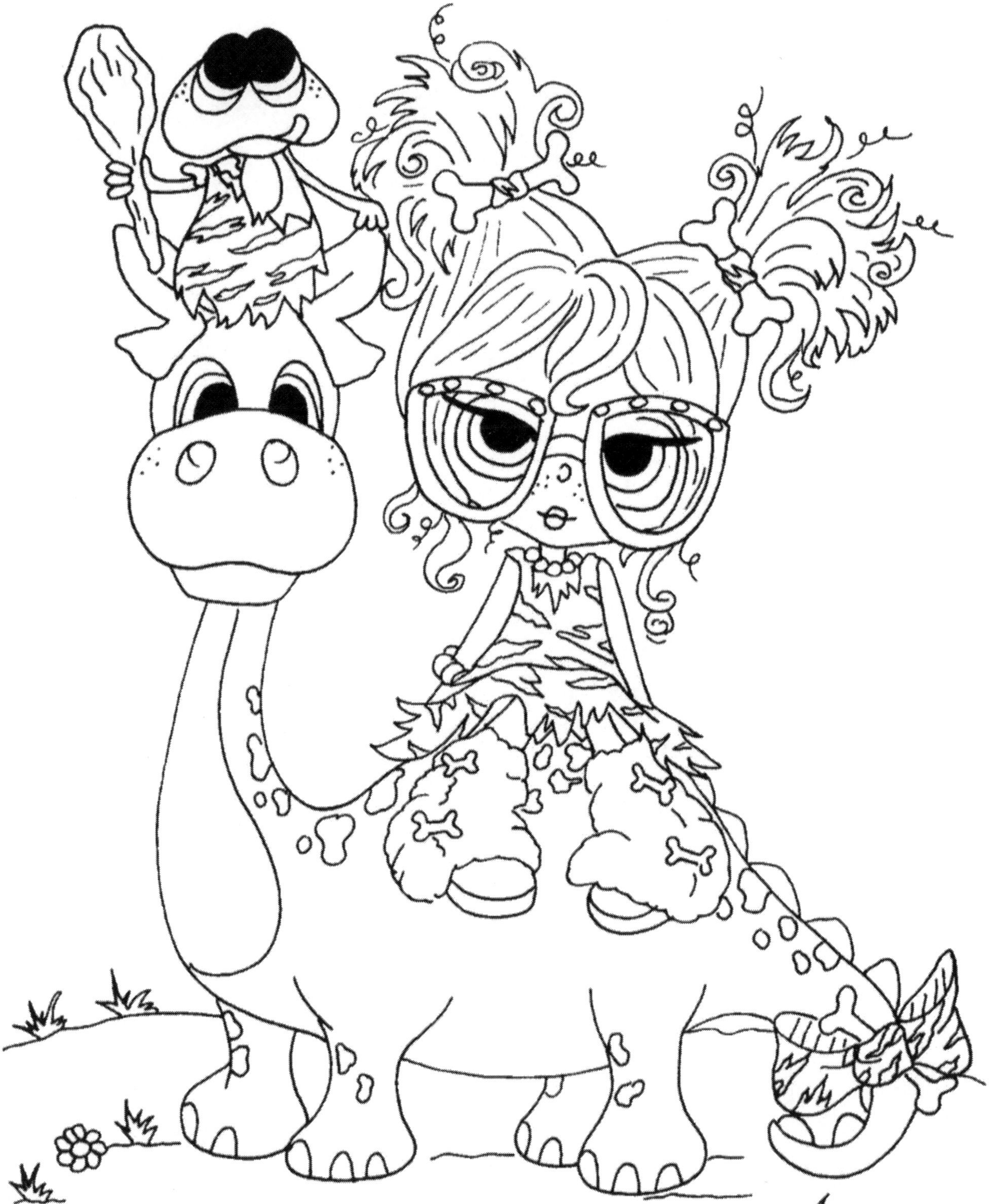

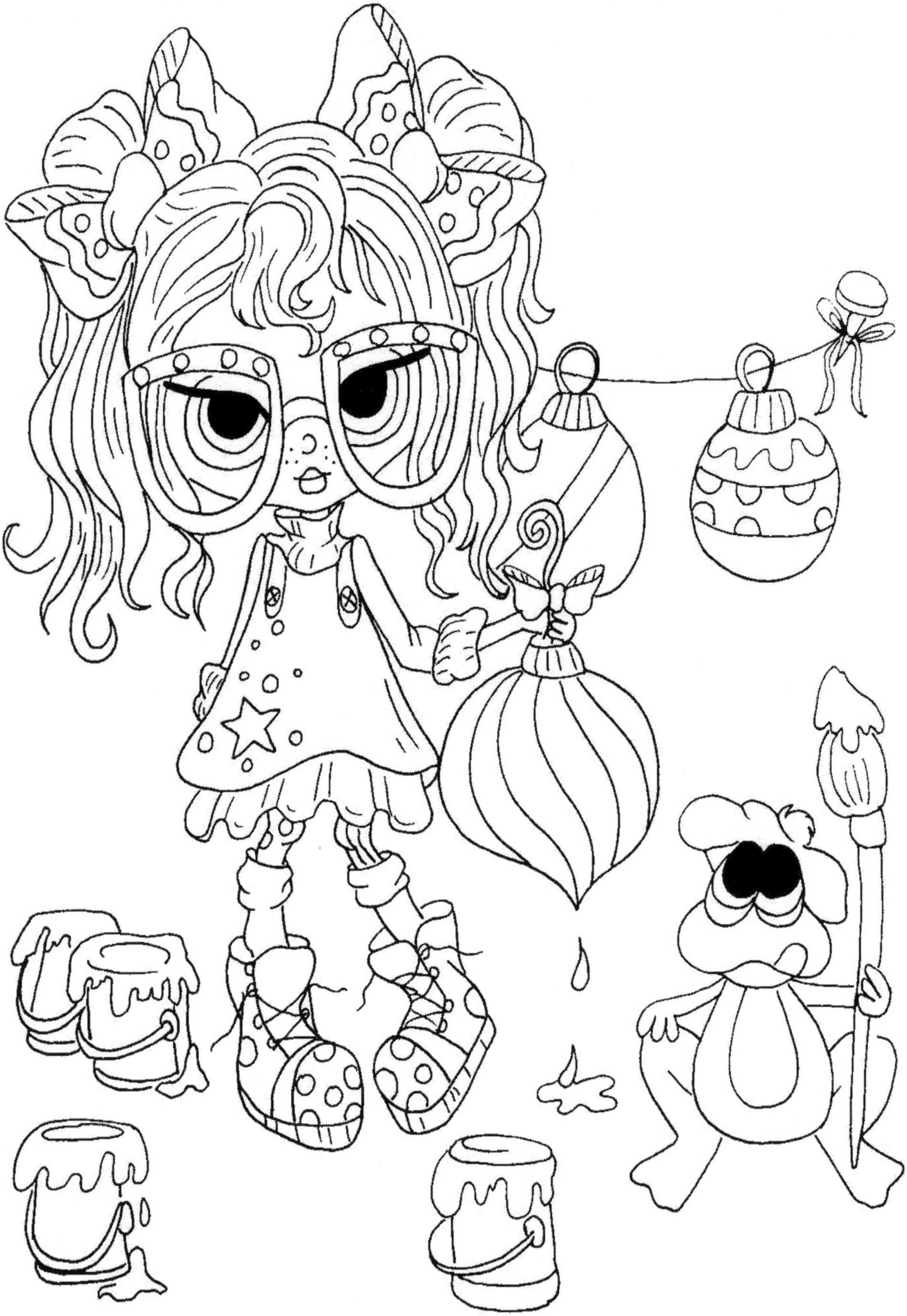

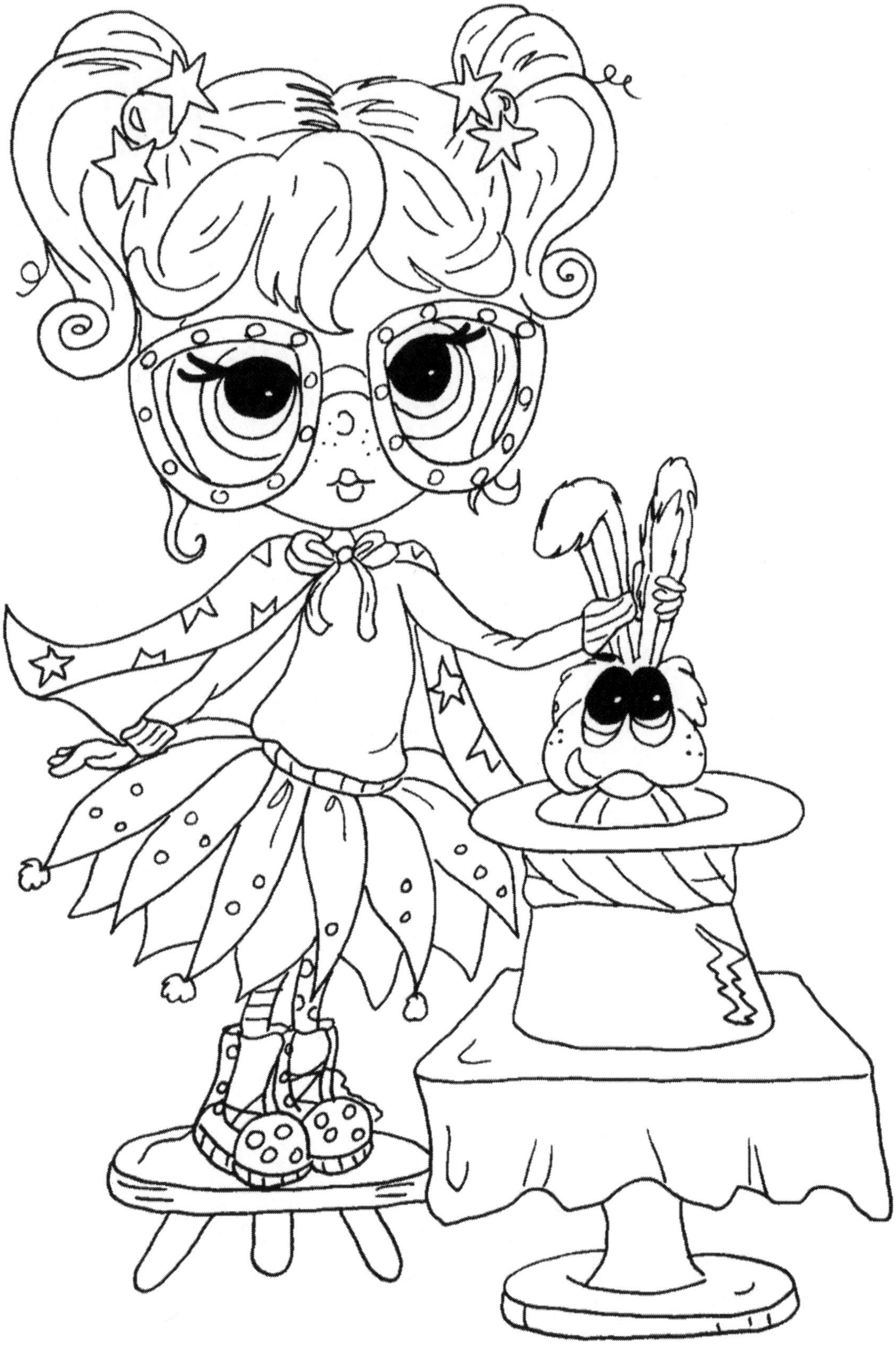

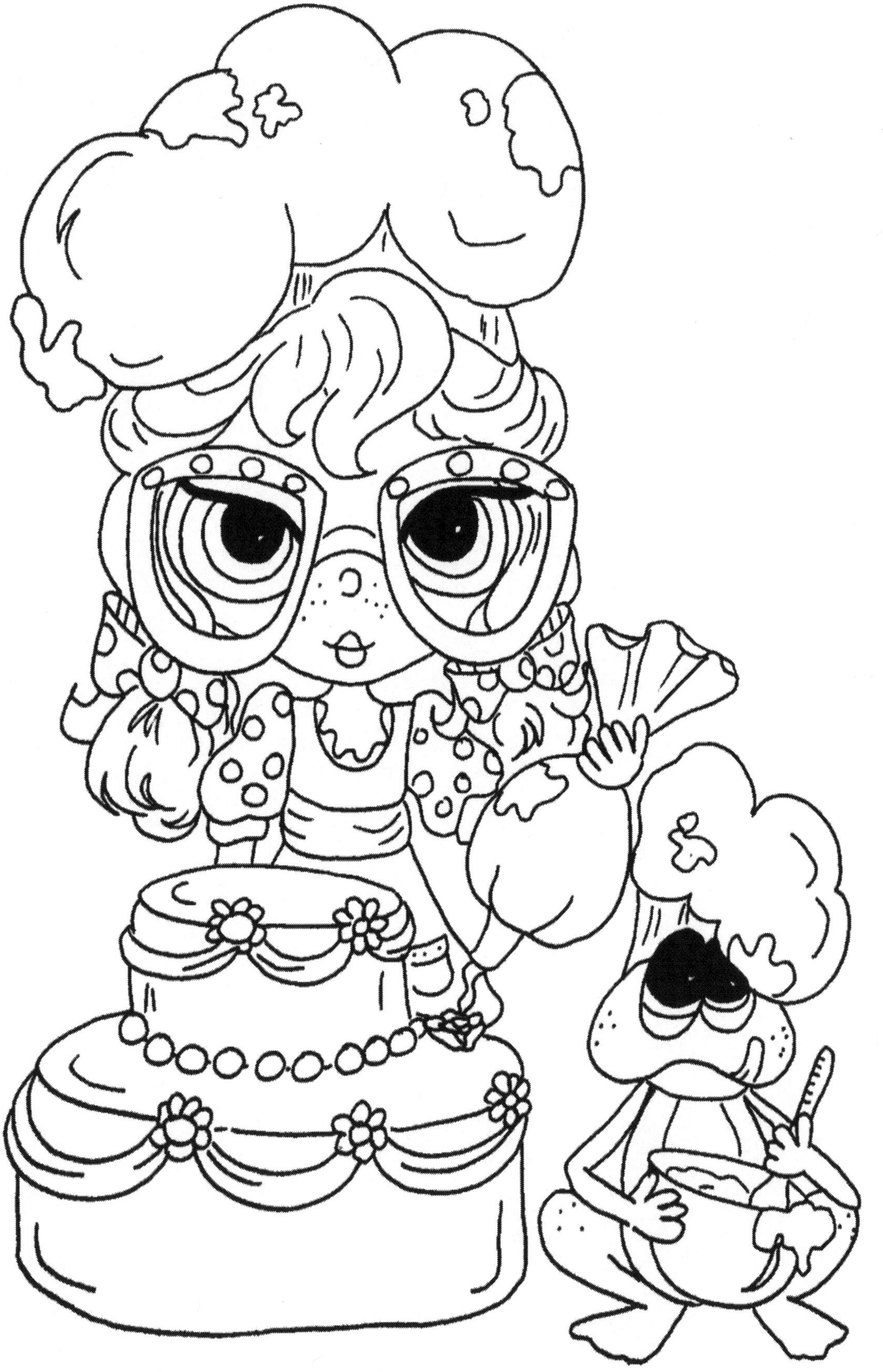

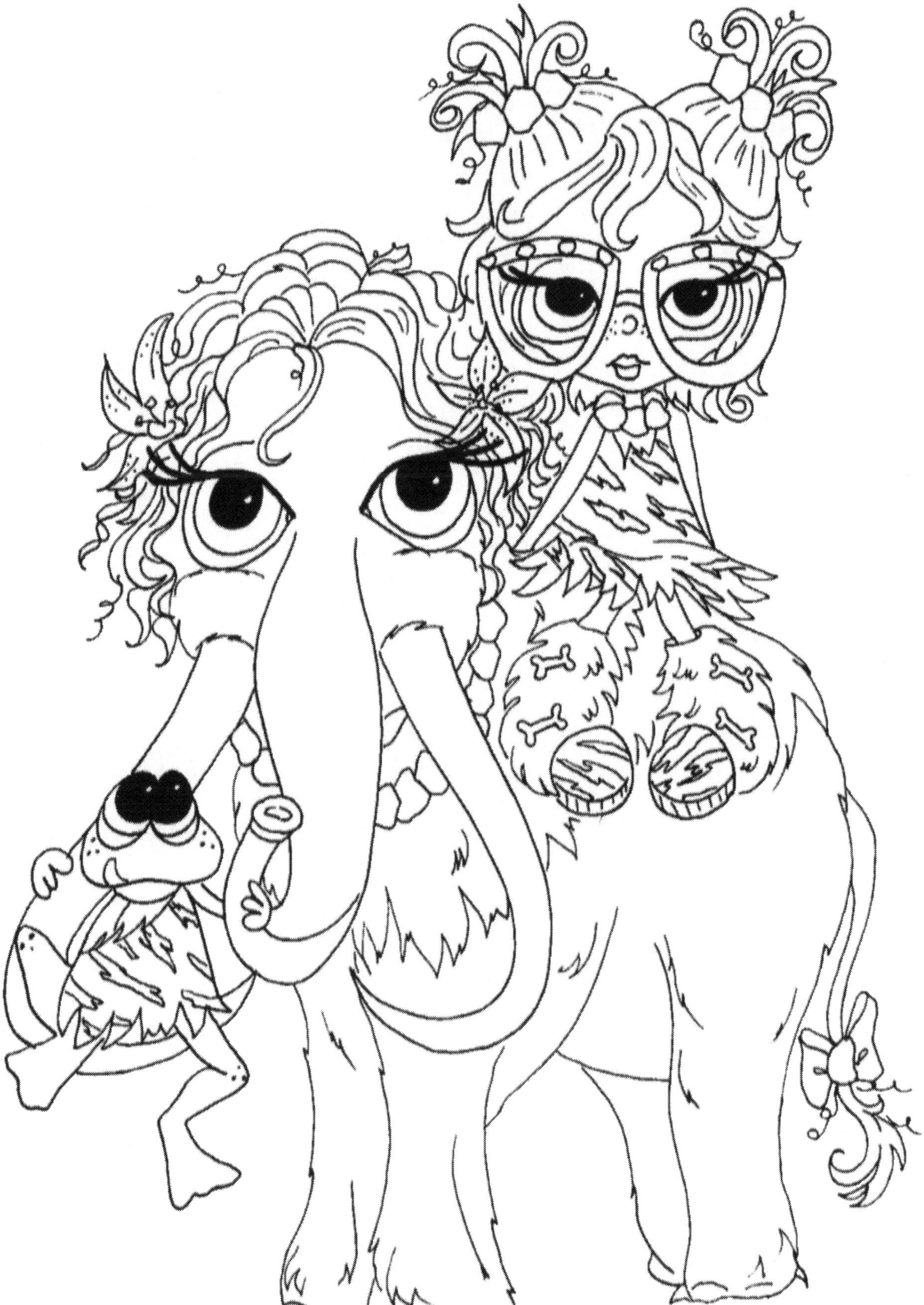

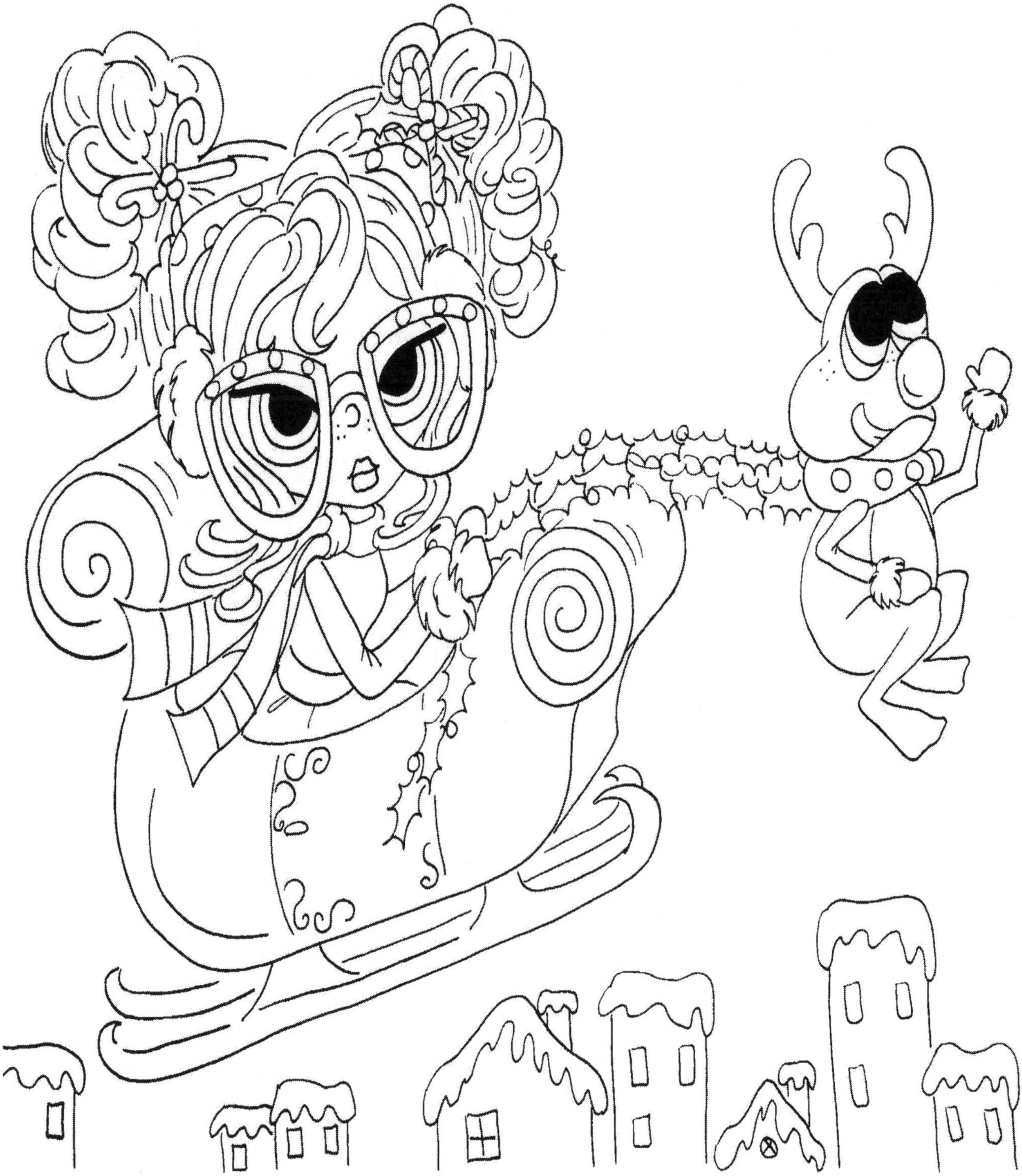

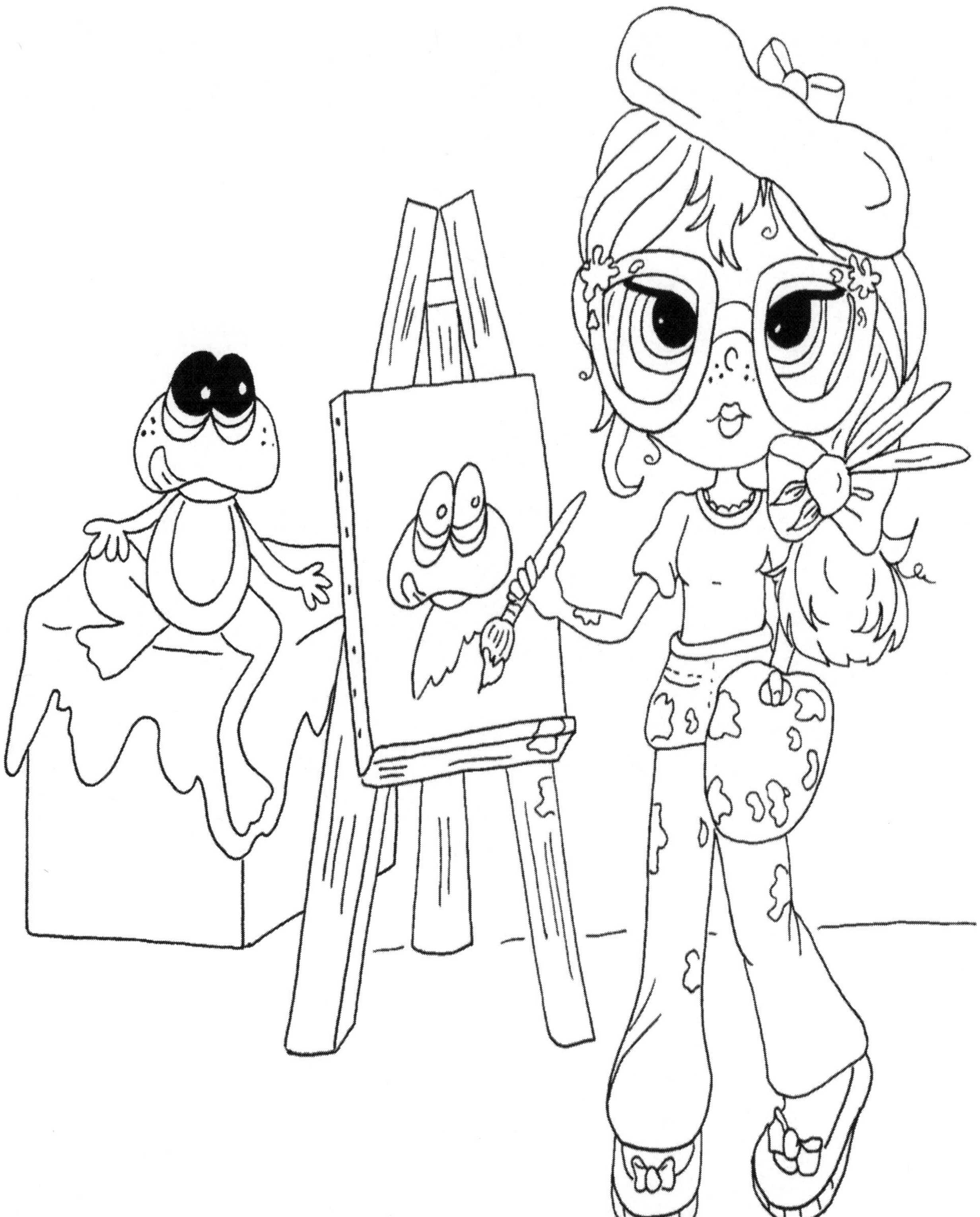

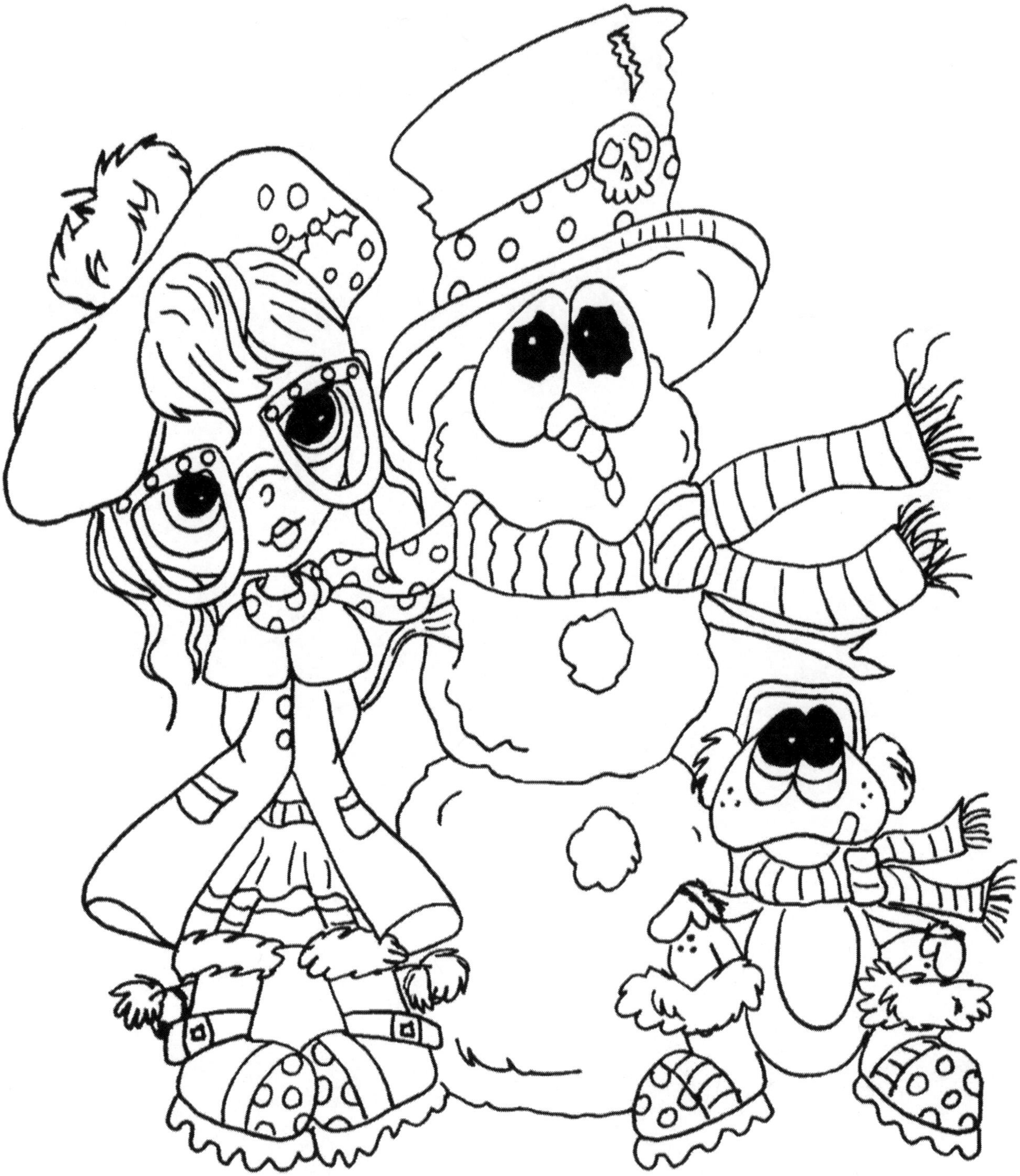

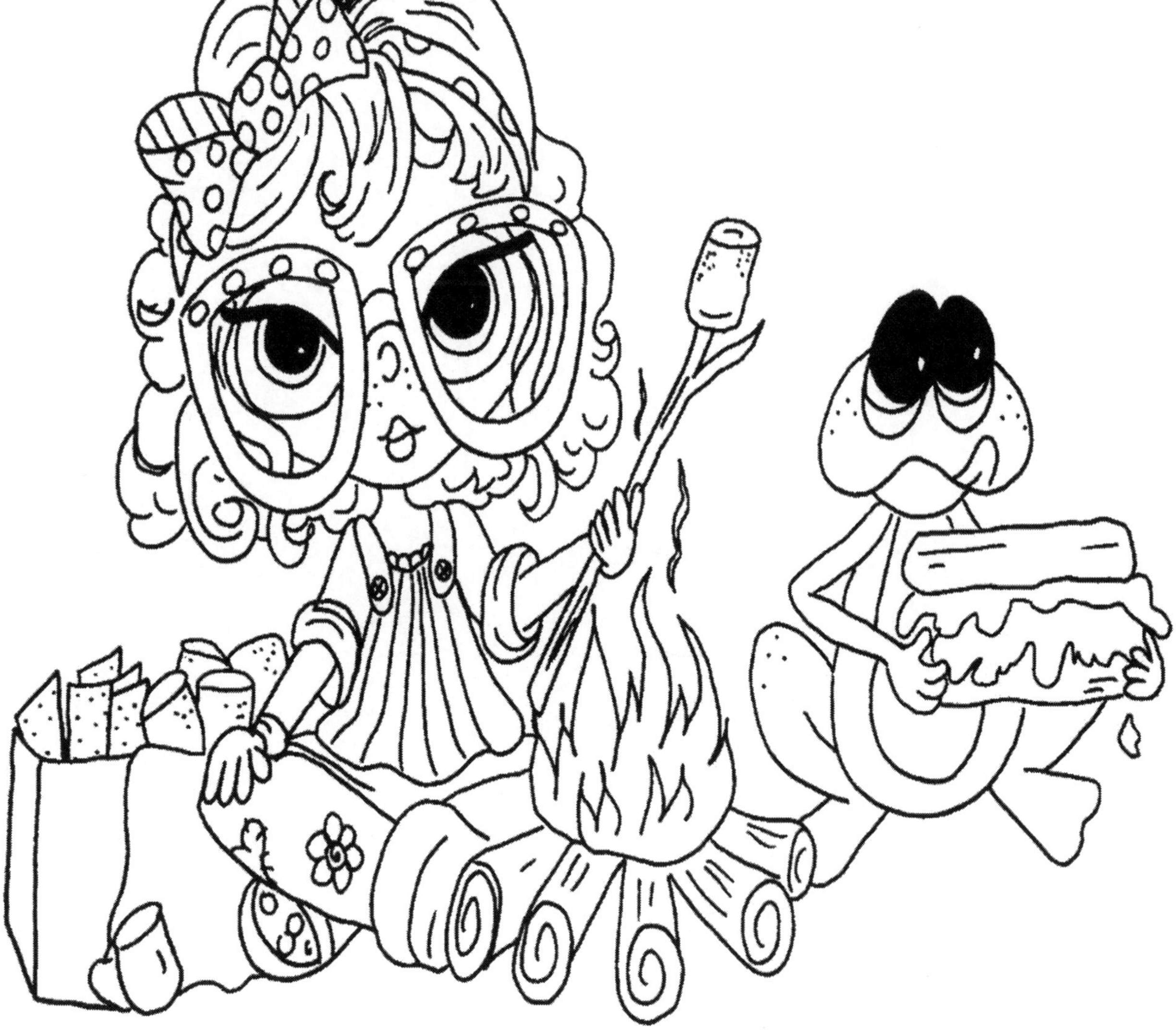

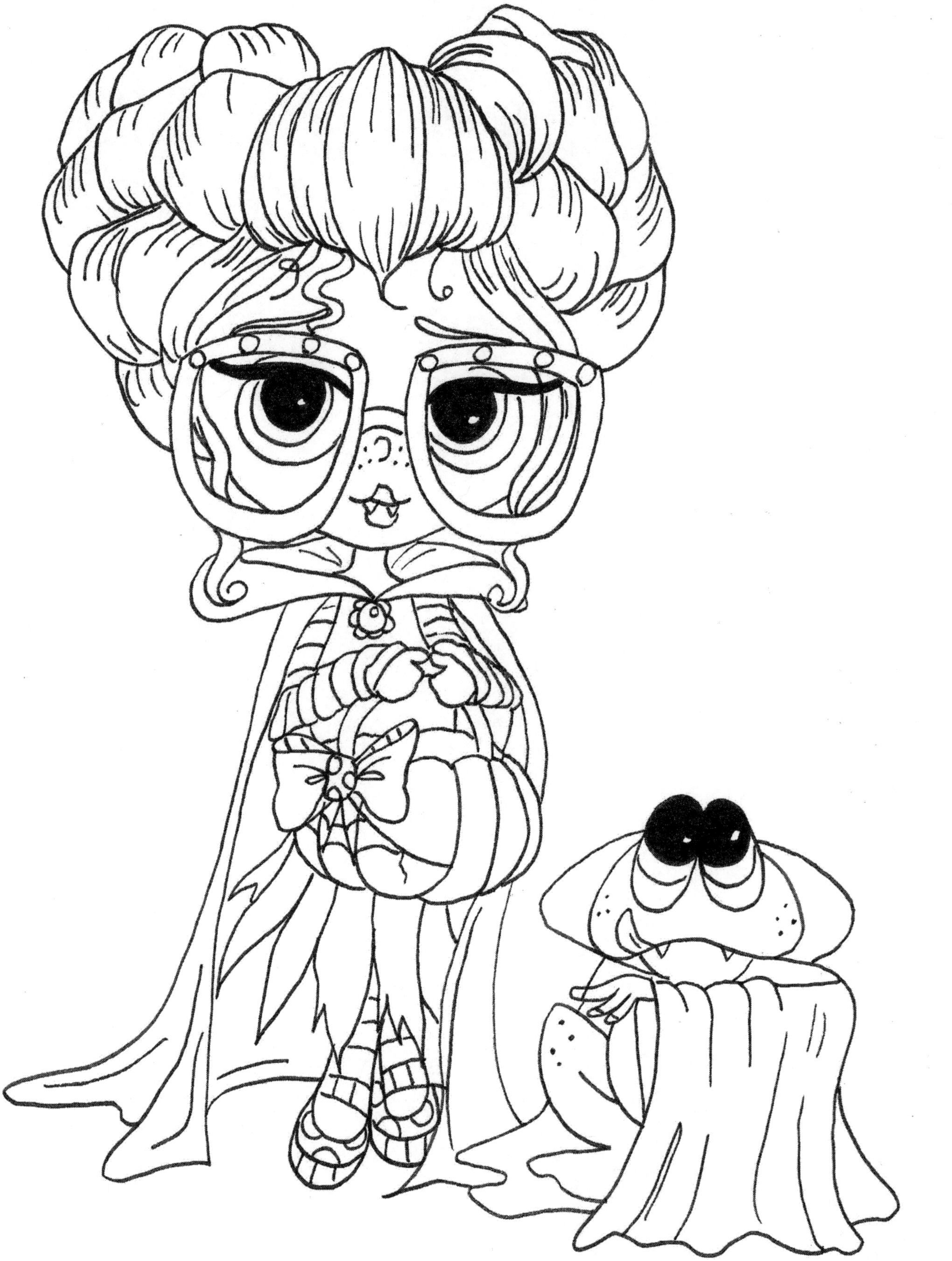

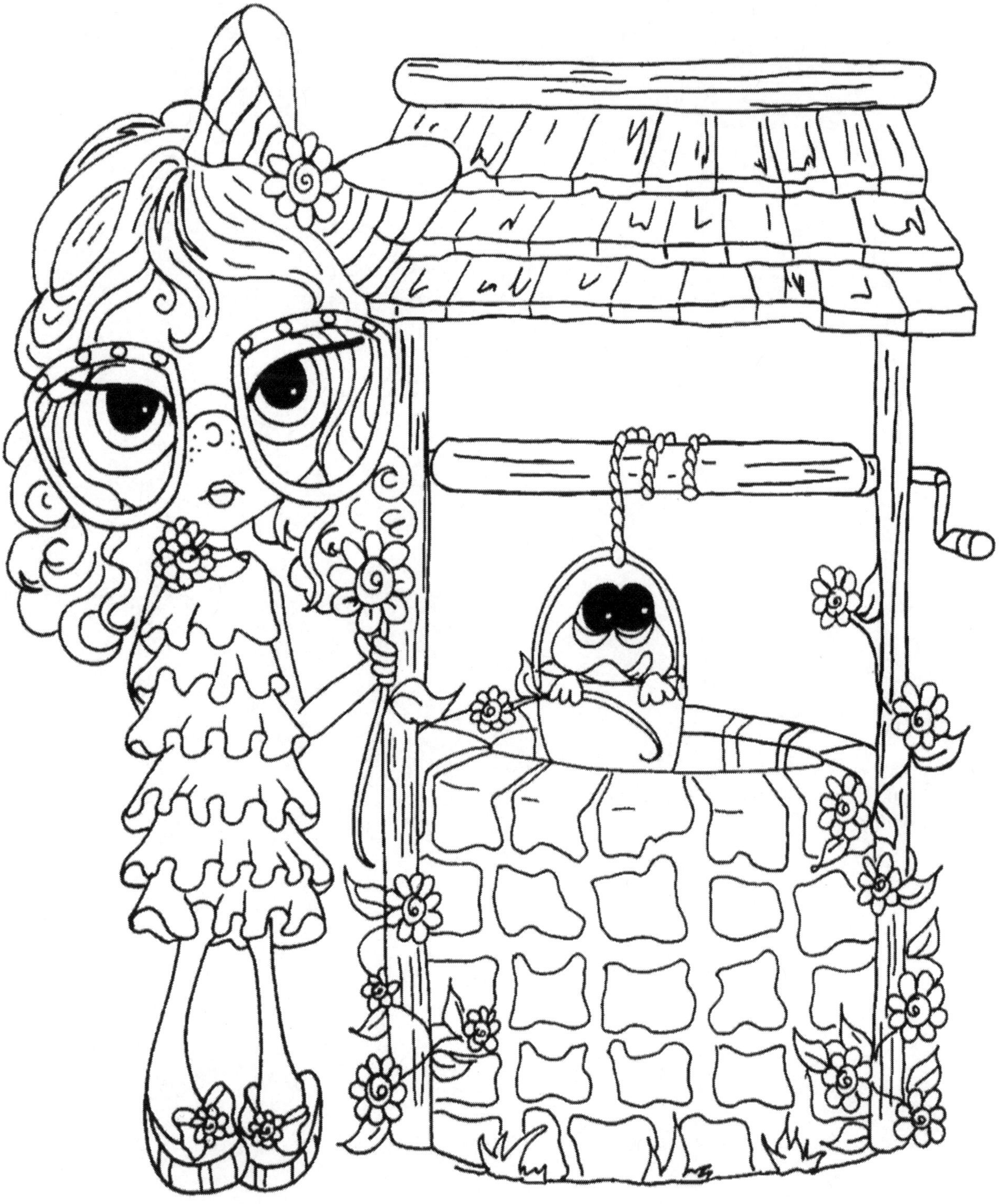

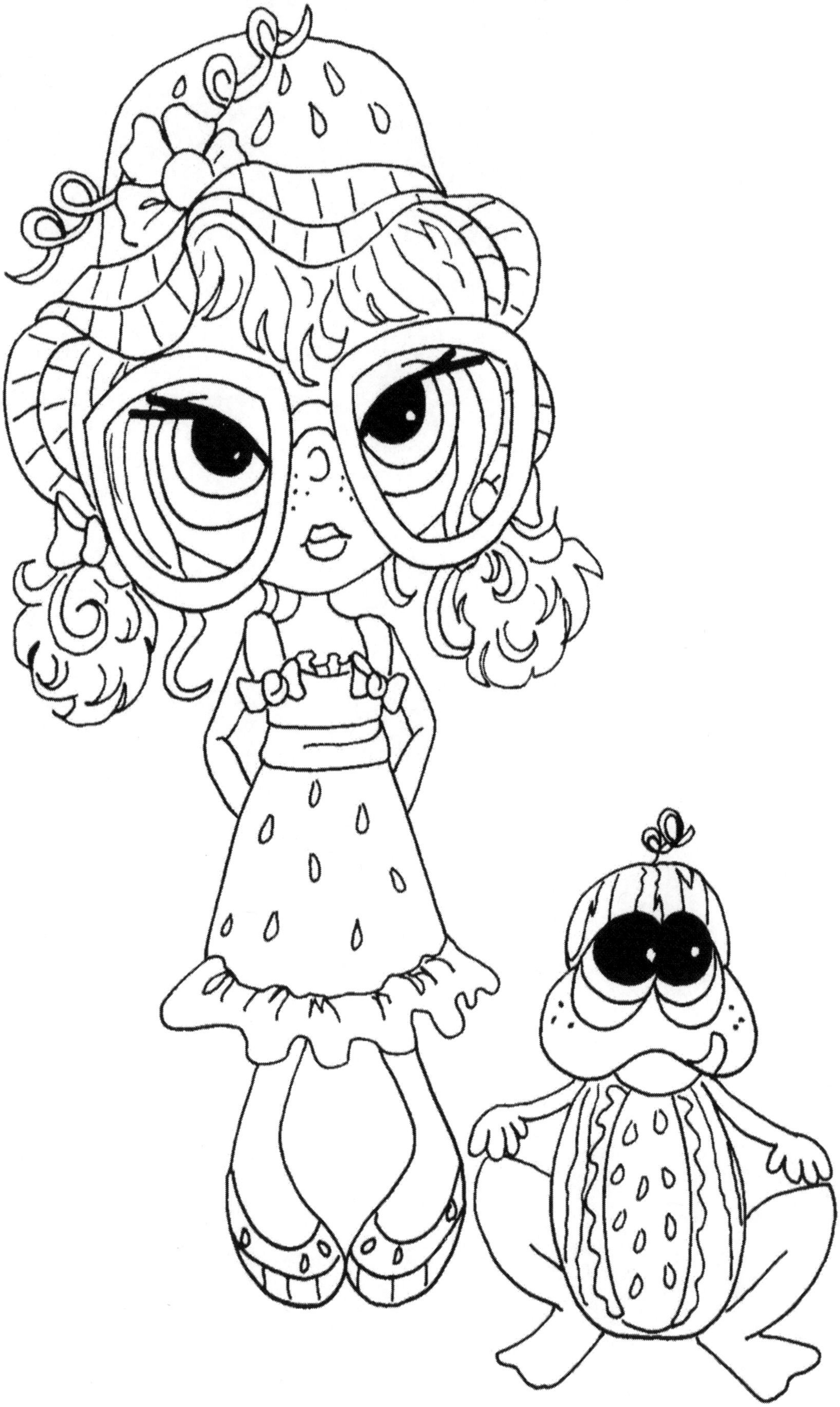

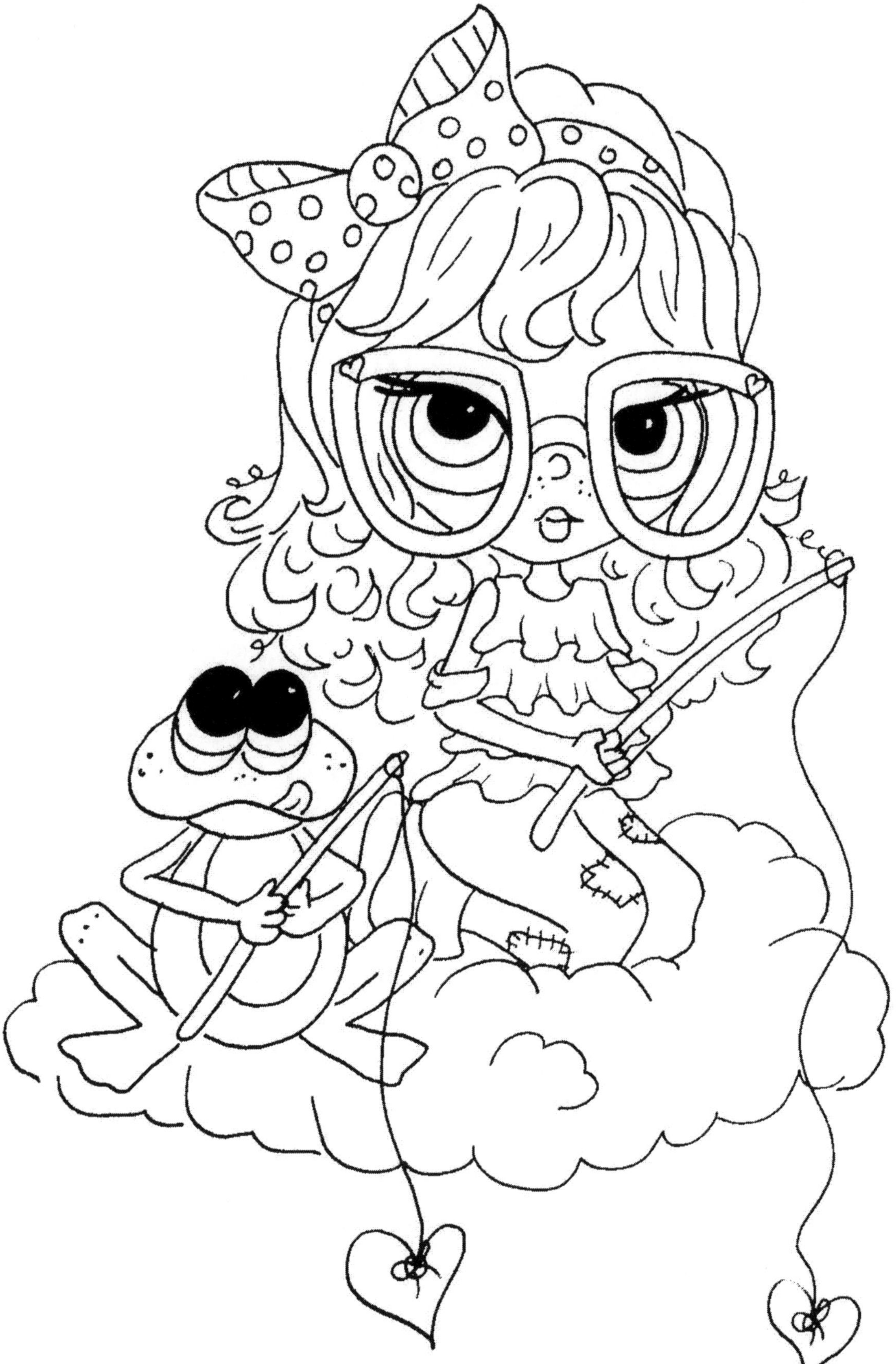

82754963R00040

Made in the USA
Lexington, KY
05 March 2018